# COMPREHENSION to 16

# Answer Book

Geoff Barton

Great Clarendon Street, Oxford OX2 6DP

Oxford University Press is a department of the University of Oxford.
It furthers the University's objective of excellence in research,
scholarship, and education by publishing worldwide in

Oxford New York

Auckland Cape Town Dar es Salaam Hong Kong Karachi
Kuala Lumpur Madrid Melbourne Mexico City Nairobi
New Delhi Shanghai Taipei Toronto

With offices in

Argentina Austria Brazil Chile Czech Republic France Greece
Guatemala Hungary Italy Japan Poland Portugal Singapore
South Korea Switzerland Thailand Turkey Ukraine Vietnam

Oxford is a registered trade mark of Oxford University Press
in the UK and in certain other countries



First published 1998 as *Comprehension to GCSE Answer Book*
Reprinted as *Comprehension to 16 Answer Book*, 2004



British Library Cataloguing in Publication Data

Data available

ISBN-13: 978-0-19-831448-6

10 9 8 7

Printed by Basingstoke Press

# Contents

## Section 2

### Broader Comparison Questions and Sample Answers



## Section 3

### Student Self-Help Sheets

# Introduction

**Comprehension to 16** has been written to prepare students for the non-fiction/media papers they will encounter in GCSE English examinations. This Answer Book is an indispensable complement to the Students' Book because it completes the process of actively teaching students how to do better in their Reading papers.

## Teaching for success

Amid a busy curriculum, examination preparation can be squeezed out until the last few lessons before mock examinations or the real thing. We can feel we've done our bit by asking students to grind through a series of past papers. But the problem with this approach is that it doesn't actively teach students what constitutes a good reading response or what a strong answer looks like.

The Answer Book was put together with this purpose in mind – to show students how to improve their responses. It isn't intended to imply that there are always definite right and wrong answers in English. Sometimes there are (more often than we let on), and sometimes there aren't. But by supplying answers in a format like this – photocopiable for student use – you'll be able to show students how they should construct and phrase their responses. In other words, students can be taught more explicitly some of the techniques for constructing successful answers.

## Comprehension to 16 and Examination Board requirements

All Examination Boards require close attention to the reading of non-fiction and media texts. Comprehension-style questions at GCSE level tend to fall into two broad types:

### 1 Shorter questions

Questions are broken down into sub-questions, each looking at a different aspect of the text in turn. Some questions will ask the student to select facts from the text, and so test straight 'factual' comprehension; other, more advanced questions ask the student to comment more broadly on the style, layout and language of the text or texts.

The **Comprehension to 16** Students' Book provides a range of questions in the shorter style; this Answer Book provides sample answers to those questions. We have annotated these to indicate strengths and weaknesses in the responses. Just as students need models for improving their writing skills, so they benefit from good model answers. Whilst you won't consider all of the sample answers perfect, I hope that you'll find them useful for making specific and active teaching points in the classroom. They are intended to help students write answers more effectively and, thus, do better in the examination.

**2 Broader questions**

These questions are of a more global kind – for instance, a single over-arching question may ask the student to compare and comment on two texts. Whilst these questions encourage students to give a fuller, perhaps more personal response, they can also appear dauntingly open-ended. Students need practice in learning how to structure their responses. We have therefore included broader questions to accompany the texts in the Students' Book, plus advice points to help students structure their responses, and some focused sample paragraphs (sometimes extracted from earlier samples from the shorter questions) to illustrate how they might write about specific topics.

The purpose in both sections is to give students a clearer understanding of what is expected of them, and greater responsibility: the photocopiable format enables them to compare their own answers with those provided here. I hope from this process students will sharpen their awareness of their own strengths and weaknesses and gain a sense of how to develop their skills.

## Self-help sheets

Finally, we felt it would be useful to include some student self-help sheets. These give direct advice on a number of relevant issues – including the old chestnut, 'How can I revise for English?' I hope that these sheets might reassure some of your students, give them practical advice, and, in turn, build their confidence.

## Conclusion

In my experience, the more we make expectations explicit to our students, the more they are likely to achieve. Hence the **Comprehension to 16** package: texts, questions, sample answers, annotations on the strengths and weaknesses of these answers, plus self-help sheets.

I'd like to think that materials like these would have helped me to do better in English at school. I hope they'll prove a real asset for students in your classroom.

*Geoff Barton*

# A note on mark schemes

While all examination boards require students to demonstrate the ability to read and analyse non-fiction and printed media texts, the mark allocation in the exam papers themselves varies from board to board.

In order to produce materials which will be useful to all GCSE students – and to those studying for Standard Grade in Scotland – **Comprehension to 16** does not aim to replicate the mark schemes of any one examination paper.

Instead, all of the comprehension-type question sections in the Students' Book are marked out of twenty marks.

The Students' Book – and the answers which appear in this Answer Book – do, however, encourage students to use the number of marks allocated to each question as a guide to the length of answer required. As a general rule, a question with just one mark needs a one-word or one-sentence answer, while a question with four or more marks needs a paragraph answer.

Every student preparing for GCSE should become familiar with the mark schemes of the particular papers they will be sitting. You, as teacher, will probably show them past papers as a matter of course. But in the meantime, the mark guidelines in **Comprehension to 16** will give your students useful practice in judging where to concentrate their time and energy during the examination itself – regardless of which papers they are sitting.

# Section 1

# Answers to Student Book questions

# Leaflets

**Text A**

## RSPCA leaflet

**1** Name one thing that donations to the RSPCA might help to pay for. (2 marks)

They might help to pay for:

- first aid and medication
- veterinary care
- 24-hour service
- a large team of inspectors.

Advice

Try not to use exactly the wording used in the leaflet. Each of these answers is a shortened or different version. Remember that you are expected to write your answer in a full sentence.

**2** At the foot of the leaflet it says 'We receive no government funding'. Why do you think it says this? (2 marks)

The sentence makes us more likely to make a donation because the charity does not receive official support.

**3** Write two sentences using your own words. In one, say what happened to Trio. In the other, say what happened to Poppy. (4 marks)

Your sentences should say something like these:

Trio was brutally treated by his owner [1 mark] and nursed by the RSPCA [1 mark]. Poppy was flushed down the toilet [1 mark] and saved by the RSPCA [1 mark].

Advice

Notice that the writer aims to get the full four marks by making four points. It is a good, clear answer.

**4** Look at the letter from Inspector Colin Strong in the centre of the leaflet. What impression do you get of him? (6 marks)

Possible points:

The photograph of Colin Strong is friendly. It shows that he likes animals.

The signature is a good personal touch, encouraging us to feel positive about the work of the RSPCA.

He shows his loyalty and commitment to the RSPCA and to animals – for example, 'I can't turn my back on all the battered, tormented and abandoned animals who need my help'.

He is obviously 'dedicated' to the job – 'on call 24 hours a day'.

He makes it sound as if the money donated will be used personally by him ('Will you give me the resources I need…?'). This makes him sound like a hero or crusader.

Advice The best answers will use short quotations from the text to support their points.

**5** How does the leaflet persuade readers to support the work of the RSPCA? You might comment upon:

- the layout
- the content
- the language (6 marks)

The layout is clear and easy to follow. It has different types of text to hold our interest – stories (Trio, Poppy, Tara) which make us feel involved in the way the animals are treated; a letter (to make us understand the work of the inspectors); photographs to illustrate the animals' suffering; a factual panel showing where our money goes.

The content is quite emotional – it features stories which make us feel involved, plus a letter asking us directly to help. The content includes specific details – names like Poppy and Barnes Hill hospital, plus facts in the shaded panel below. These help us to take the work of the charity seriously.

The language is quite brutal in describing how animals can be treated (e.g. 'punish', 'smash', 'threw'). The language used to describe the RSPCA is very different: 'the loving attentions of RSPCA staff', 'weeks of tender, expert care'. The tone of Inspector Strong's letter is quite informal addressing the reader directly as 'you' and building up a feeling of respect between the reader and the writer.

Advice Remember that high-level answers focus on specific words.

# Leaflets

**Text B**

## Greenpeace leaflet

**1** How did the Greenpeace organization begin? (1 mark)

It began when some protesters sailed a boat into a nuclear test zone in 1971.

**2** Name two issues that Greenpeace campaigns about. (1 mark)

It campaigns about global warming and whaling.

Advice

A clear answer. It might have said, instead, rainforests, ozone levels, toxic pollution, and nuclear testing.

**3** In the description of the campaign against whaling, the leaflet says that Greenpeace 'put whaling back on the public agenda'. Say, in your own words, what you think this means. (2 marks)

It means that people started to think and talk about the issue of whale-hunting again.

Advice

A good, clear answer: it restates the information without repeating the words in the text.

**4** The last page of the leaflet gives a brief history of the planet Earth. What point is this passage making? (4 marks)

The comparison of the World with a human life helps us to see what humans have done. It shows how briefly human beings have had any role on the planet and yet we have 'made a rubbish tip of paradise'. The timescale illustrates how damaging our brief time on Earth has been.

The text also helps us to feel involved with Greenpeace's arguments. By comparing the Earth to a person, we are more likely to feel sympathy for it – to feel ashamed of what we have done. The final paragraph lists in more detail the destruction humans have committed.

Advice

This is an impressive answer because it shows an understanding of what the writer is trying to achieve. It is clearly expressed and uses a supporting quotation. It is a high-level answer.

**5** Look more closely at the design of the leaflet. Write a paragraph about the use of:

- images
- headlines
- subheadings

How successful is the layout in grabbing and holding the reader's attention? (6 marks)

The design uses a strong visual image on the cover – a man holding a seal in a net. On first sight, the man could be hurting the seal, and perhaps this is a weakness because it runs the risk of being misinterpreted. But its main point is to show us that someone doing something – saving an animal – is more important than talking about it. The image, in other words, illustrates what the slogan is saying.

The headlines are clear and factual. The writer chooses to repeat the word 'action' to emphasize the way Greenpeace is about doing things rather than discussion. I think perhaps the repetition of action throughout the text is a bit too much.

Subheadings help to break the text up and keep us reading.

One weakness in the overall design is that it feels a bit disjointed. Lots of small images make it feel a bit cluttered, and perhaps a stronger, larger single image would prove more powerful.

Overall the design gives the leaflet a feeling of urgency and realism.

Advice

This isn't such a strong answer. It feels short of detailed examples in places (for example when discussing the subheadings). But it has some impressive moments, and is often well phrased (e.g. 'a feeling of urgency'). One strong point in the answer is the way the writer has opinions about the leaflet, saying exactly what he or she thinks.

**6** Does the language of the leaflet seem straightforward or difficult? Is it simple or high-level? Which parts are easiest to follow and which cause difficulty? Write a brief paragraph commenting on the language of the leaflet. (6 marks)

The language level overall feels straightforward and accessible. It contains technical terms – global warming, toxic pollution, effluent – but these help us to feel that Greenpeace knows what it is talking about. If they just said 'lots of horrible waste' it would sound childish and unconvincing.

Sometimes the text feels more informal and more directly addressed to the reader – for example, 'We're not asking you to sail...'. The lighthearted tone of this is good, a contrast to the more factual style of other parts.

Advice

This is a very brief answer, but it makes perceptive points about the language. The final comment is especially good – about the difference in tone across the leaflet. The writer could explore this further.

The writer could also look at the question of audience. The use of technical terms in the leaflet suggests it is aimed at educated readers.

# Leaflets comparison

## Healthy Eating leaflets

**1** What reasons do the two leaflets give to persuade us to think more about our diets? (4 marks)

Thinking more about our diets will help prevent future problems, such as coronary heart disease; give children the essential vitamins and minerals they need; keep our bodies in good working order; give us energy; help children's growth.

Advice

This isn't an easy question because neither leaflet gives many reasons and some of them seem to overlap a bit. Your answer could include any of the points above. To get full marks it would probably be wise to try to find four reasons. Notice how the writer uses semicolons to separate the different parts of the answer. This technique makes it clearer for the examiner to follow the answer.

**2** Write down three facts you learn from the leaflets. Then write down three pieces of advice you learn. (6 marks)

Three facts from the leaflets are:

1 Children's teeth are most at risk from tooth decay.
2 Meat and dark-green vegetables are rich sources of iron.
3 Bread, cereals and potatoes provide us with energy, starch, fibre, vitamins and minerals.

Three pieces of advice from the leaflets are:

1 Parents should only buy the food that they want their children to eat.
2 Parents should encourage their children not to eat meals in front of the television.
3 People should experiment with eating low-fat versions of dairy products like milk, yoghurt and cheese.

Advice

The writer lists each block of three answers as separate points. This is fine because it is a clear way of giving the examiner the information. There are other facts and pieces of advice that could be listed. Notice that the answer above contains examples from both leaflets, not just one.

**3** Compare the two leaflets and describe what you notice about:

- who they are aimed at
- what they say
- how they are set out
- the language they use

(10 marks)

The first leaflet is about children but it is not aimed at children. It is aimed at parents. It says, for example, 'Give your children fruit...'. It is intended to educate parents. The Waitrose leaflet is also aimed at adults. It sounds more like a partnership between writer and reader: 'Should we avoid certain foods altogether?'

The advice in both leaflets is similar – for example, the need to cut down sugar and fat. The Tesco leaflet places more stress, of course, on the needs of young children and summarizes its advice on the 'tips' section. The Waitrose leaflet gives more technical information. It talks about 'kilojoules' and 'kilocalories' and shows how to read nutrition labels. This is another sign that it is aimed completely at adults.

The Tesco leaflet has a brighter, more eye-catching design, perhaps because it is talking about children's habits. The illustrations have the feel of cartoons, and the 'tips' headline is made up from children's magnetic letters. This makes it all feel informal and quite lighthearted. The Waitrose leaflet uses attractive images of fruit, vegetables and fish. Its main pages are dominated by the plate of different healthy foodstuffs. The design makes it clear and quite informal, but not at all lighthearted.

The language in the Tesco leaflet is very direct. It tells readers what they should do (the imperative form of the verb): 'Only buy…'; 'Always grill…'. This gives it a bit of a bossy tone. The Waitrose leaflet seems less direct. It uses verbs like 'Try to…' and 'Opt for…'. This makes it feel less like an order and more like a suggestion. The Waitrose leaflet also uses 'We' a lot, emphasizing that this is a partnership between the store and its customers.

**Advice**

Notice how the answer has been written in paragraphs which correspond to the bullet-points of the question. This will help the examiner to mark it quickly. The answer is good. There are other points to be made (for example, there is nothing in the design paragraph about text size, font styles, use of spaces, use of colour, and so on), but it is a good answer. The attention to the language is particularly good – some really detailed comments on the words used in both texts and a good discussion of the tone of each leaflet.

# Reportage

## Text A

### Newspaper report

**1** Why do Roderick and Arabella have a fox iced onto their wedding cake? (2 marks)

The fox is a reminder that they first met at a hunt and that hunting has remained an important part of their lives.

**Advice** You only need to make one of these two points.

**2** What evidence is there that foxes are clever? (2 marks)

One hunter says that foxes run through areas of country which smell more, so that the hunting dogs find it difficult to follow the foxes' scent.

**3** Why did Daphne Rickerts first join the League Against Cruel Sports? (2 marks)

She once saw the cruelty of hunting when a hare was killed close to her house.

**4** The headline to the article is, 'Different classes who are brought together by the thrill of the chase'. Write a paragraph about some of the different types of people who are involved in fox-hunting – as hunters and as hunt monitors. (6 marks)

The writer describes the 'classlessness' of the hunt – the fact that anyone can become involved whatever their background. She presents quite a range of people.

Roderick and Arabella Moore are barristers. The fact that they have £300 riding boots suggests that they are wealthy. Both of the names suggest that they come from a higher social class.

Marilyn Husbands describes herself as 'terribly ordinary'. The use of the word 'terribly' makes her sound as if she is from a higher social class. She runs a chain of dress shops.

Keith Colbert is an electrician from London and the writer describes him as saying he is 'gutted'. This feels quite different from the language used by the hunters themselves. His role in the hunt is different too – he doesn't ride horses: he puts the terriers into the holes.

There is also a lollipop lady – Penny Rendle.

The hunt monitors seem quite ordinary, although Daphne feels like an upper class name. Their former jobs were with the Inland Revenue and as a draughtsman.

The headline seems right – the hunt involves a wide range of people.

Advice

This is a good answer because it is systematic. It answers the question step-by-step, showing that the writer mentions a range of types of people. It looks at the language (including people's names) to support ideas about the backgrounds people come from. It avoids saying that people are 'posh' or 'common' – which students sometimes do, and which can reduce the discussion to a lower tone.

The answer could emphasize one point more: the people who actually ride the horses do seem more wealthy, from a higher class. The electrician does not actually seem equal to the others. He is told what to do, and has to take orders. He almost seems like a servant of the real hunters.

**5** Is the writer of the article neutral, or does she seem to be on the side of either the hunters or hunt monitors? Support your response with specific examples. (8 marks)

I think the writer pokes fun at the hunters a bit. When she describes Marilyn Husbands saying, 'I'm terribly ordinary', she adds in brackets: 'three times'. This suggests someone who is a bit of a bore. She also quotes one of the hunters saying 'Oh no, she's fallen orf'. This seems to be mocking the upper class language they use. Her last paragraph says, 'I didn't hear one single "Tally ho!" all day'. Again, I think this is poking fun at the hunters – showing what she expected them to be like – even though she seems to be making no judgement about 'right, wrong, nice or nasty'.

The writer seems quite neutral about the hunt monitors. Some writers might have labelled them 'hunt saboteurs' which would have made them feel much more negative. She seems to show that they are different from the main hunters – for example, they drive a 'battered old vehicle'. This hints that they are here because of their strong beliefs, whereas the main hunters are here as part of their wealthy lifestyle. She describes how Daphne became a hunt monitor (after seeing a hare ripped apart), and this makes us feel sympathy for Daphne, feel on her side. The hunt monitors are shown laughing at the hunters, when the hunt seems to fall apart. Again, this makes us feel as if we are on the hunt monitors' side. But the last paragraph seems a bit far-fetched. Ken says: 'We'll never get a perfect world while humans are in it'. Some writers might have poked fun at this, but Lynne Wallis quotes it without comment. This shows that she is either neutral, or even on the side of the hunt monitors.

Advice

This has a good clear feel to it, and provides plenty of supporting evidence for each point. The point about the 'Tally Ho!' in the last paragraph of the main article isn't very clearly made. It isn't obvious why this should be poking fun at the hunters. The second half of the answer, about the hunt monitors, is very convincing.

# Reportage

**Text B**

## Eyewitness account

**1** Give one reason why George Orwell does not want to kill the elephant. (2 marks)

Possible answers could be:

He simply does not want to.

He particularly dislikes the thought of killing a large animal.

He worries about what the elephant's owner will think.

You should put down only one of these.

**2** George Orwell is worried about what the Burmese spectators might think of him. What is he afraid of? (2 marks)

He is afraid that they will think he is scared and that they will laugh if he makes a mistake.

**3** Why does Orwell not stay to watch the death of the elephant? (2 marks)

He cannot stand it – the sight is too upsetting.

B

**4** Many readers are disturbed by George Orwell's attitude to the Burmese people around him. Write a paragraph about the way he describes them, and his attitude to them. (6 marks)

The description seems quite racist. He describes the 'yellow faces' of the crowd, and emphasizes how isolated he feels by saying 'A white man mustn't be frightened in front of "natives".' He describes the Burmese people through labels – 'natives' – rather than making them seem individual or human. He also suggests that their response to the shooting of the elephant is barbaric, comparing them to an audience waiting for a 'theatre curtain to go up'. This makes them sound unfeeling and uncaring – they are just there for the entertainment. When the gun goes off he describes the 'devilish roar of glee' from the crowd. The word 'devilish' shows his clear dislike of the people and, in particular, the way they are enjoying this spectacle. At the end he describes the way the people scavenge over the body – 'they had stripped his body almost to the bones by the afternoon'. He seems to find this distasteful.

**Advice**

This answer gets to the heart of the description. It has plenty of examples – including the description at the end of people looting the body. The answer focuses well on specific words like 'devilish' and 'natives', and then shows how these are presenting the Burmese people in a particular way. It is a very good answer.

**5** How does George Orwell use language to help the reader to visualize the death of the elephant? What feelings do you think he expects us to have? (8 marks)

He gives us quite a long build-up before shooting the elephant. This builds anticipation and suspense – will he get it right or not? This helps us to feel more involved in the text. When he fires the bullet, the pace of the text almost seems to slow down. He describes each stage the elephant goes through in death. He uses words which make the elephant seem different – suddenly frail – 'stricken, shrunken, immensely old'. This shows that he is seeing the elephant as something of an innocent victim, something which could not hope to fight back. When Orwell says 'the frightful impact of the bullet' he again suggests something unfair in this process – as if the elephant could never have a chance against the efficiency and power of the weapon.

He shows the enormous bulk of the elephant as it dies, comparing it to a 'huge rock toppling'. This would seem a neutral description except that in his next paragraph Orwell gives details of the elephant fighting for its life – 'long rattling gasps'. This makes us feel powerful sympathy for what is happening to the elephant. The description of the blood 'like red velvet' makes the blood feel thick and red, and almost unreal.

The description is quite emotional, saying that the elephant is 'in great agony', and this is contrasted with the scurrying haste of the people to get at him. Repetition of 'dreadful' and later use of the word 'tortured' leave us in no doubt that we should be feeling sympathy for the dying elephant.

Advice

This answer gives plenty of examples, but it seems to become a bit of a list. A better answer might have a paragraph looking at the description of the death; then a separate paragraph discussing how Orwell shapes our emotional response. This way the answer would feel more systematic, and better organized.

# Reportage comparison 1

## Reporting styles

**1** 'The hunters in the first text are looking forward to the hunt.'
'George Orwell hates the idea of killing the elephant.'
Find a quotation from each text which supports these statements.
(2 marks)

There are several possibilities. Perhaps the clearest quotations are:

'Their backs are ramrod straight, their faces set – perhaps in anticipation of thrills and kills ahead.'

'I did not want to shoot the elephant.'

Advice

Remember that with a question like this, you only need to copy out the relevant quotation. Be careful to copy it correctly and place it in speech marks to show that it is a quotation, not your own words.

**2** Write down one clue that the first text is a piece of journalism.
(2 marks)

There are several possible clues:

- layout – the use of headlines, strap-line, short paragraphs, columns
- language – such as the use of labels ('Roderick, 27, is…')
- the fact that the writer generally avoids saying 'I' and focuses on the comments of the people at the hunt.

**3** Write down one clue that George Orwell's text is personal. (2 marks)

The chief clue is the repeated use of 'I'.

Advice

Remember not to write too much for questions 2 and 3 – they are worth two marks each. The bulk of your marks will be gained on question 4, so leave plenty of time for that.

**4** What differences do you notice in the way the two texts are written?
You might comment upon:

- which is easier to follow
- which is more emotional
- what we learn about the writer from each text
- how their use of language differs. (14 marks)

Advice

Remember that some of these points will be personal opinion. Say what you think and support your comments with quotations.

Both texts are quite easy to follow. Lynne Wallis's article presents a picture of a group of people, whereas George Orwell deals with his own story and the emotions he feels. His text is therefore more direct because we trace what he sees and thinks. His text is also more emotional. Lynne Wallis stays quite neutral about what she thinks of hunting. She says, 'right, wrong, nice or nasty' at the end of her article, but doesn't say which of the words best describes her feelings. She pokes fun at the language of the hunters a bit – 'she's fallen orf' – which could suggest that she's on the side of the hunt monitors. But she avoids revealing her feelings directly.

George Orwell's emotions are much more in evidence. In the first half of his description he says, 'I was not afraid in the ordinary sense'. This is because he knows he is being watched, so he tries to hide his fear. Later in the extract he uses emotive words like 'frightful' and 'painfully' to show us that the elephant is suffering. George Orwell obviously sympathizes with the elephant's pain strongly because he says 'I felt that I had got to put an end to that dreadful noise'.

We learn little about Lynne Wallis from her text. We know that she gets involved with the hunt, riding 'Tonka', but we don't learn much more about her. Orwell, on the other hand, shows us his attitude to the local people. He seems racist – for example when he talks about 'the devilish roar of glee'. We also see George Orwell's feelings of horror as he watches the elephant die.

As a result of these differences, the writers' use of language is different. The newspaper report has plenty of description of the day's events, and they are described in fairly straightforward terms. The writer starts by focusing on one person, showing what he is like – 'spruced up in hacking jacket, pristine breeches and a pair of £300 "mahogany top" riding boots'. The use of the phrase 'spruced up' is quite informal, whereas 'pristine' is a more formal term, so in some ways the text is quite mixed.

George Orwell's writing style often has great simplicity, as in 'it was perfectly clear to me what I ought to do'. He says, 'The rifle was a beautiful German thing with cross-hair sights'. 'Thing' is a very informal, imprecise word to use, and 'cross-hair sights' feels like a technical term. When he describes the death of the elephant he uses language which is very straightforward, but full of emotion – like 'agony' and 'dreadful'. The text holds our interest because George Orwell uses a variety of sentence types – longer ones and shorter ones to create a contrast.

**Advice**

This is a good answer but the student needs to spell out why the quotation is racist by focusing on the use of the word 'devilish'. The student also needs to explain more about George Orwell's feelings of horror – a quotation would be useful. Other points are made which aren't supported with quotations (for example, about sentence length in the Orwell extract – a good point, but it needs proof). The answer has some excellent insights (for example noticing the formal and informal features of language), but it would be useful to have more detail about the language. For example, you might comment on:

- the shorter paragraphs in the first text – to hold readers' interest and make it easier to read. Text B goes into greater detail – it is more descriptive and has longer, more detailed paragraphs
- the frequent use of 'I' in the second text to make it more personal.

Text A has comments from various sources – it is gathering views from a range of people. Text B expresses George Orwell's view.

Text A uses the present tense: 'It's 7.10 am on Saturday…'. This makes it feel immediate, as if the writer is there at the hunt. Text B is in the past tense: 'The crowd grew very still…'. It gives the impression of the writer reflecting on something he has seen earlier.

# Reportage comparison 2

## Tabloid and broadsheet journalism

**1** Say, in a sentence, what happened to Ian and Stuart Middle. (2 marks)

They became ill in a water-filled quarry because they rose too quickly to the surface and got the bends.

**2** Why did the pilot decide to fly under the Menai bridge? (2 marks)

He aimed to keep the brothers' suffering to a minimum. The higher he flew, the more pain they would be in.

**3** Look at the headlines for each story. Which one do you think works best? Write a short paragraph saying why. (4 marks)

Advice

Write what you believe. The headline of text A has more dramatic words – 'dash', 'saves'. The headline of text B makes you more likely to want to read the story – its language is less dramatic, but it tells you that the pilot flew beneath the bridge, which grabs our attention.

It is important to say what you think and to justify your response by referring closely to the language of the text.

**4** Look at the first paragraph of each version. Write about the differences you notice. (4 marks)

Text A has the phrase 'wave hopped' which makes the flight sound highly dangerous and daring. Text B has a more dramatic first paragraph though, because it also mentions that the pilot flew under power cables. Text A gives the outline of the whole story in clear, direct language. Text B uses higher level vocabulary – 'potentially lethal' – suggesting that its audience may be more educated. It has a longer first paragraph, giving more detail.

Advice

This would be a better answer if it was better organized. At present it feels a bit jumbled. Perhaps the writer should break it into two paragraphs – one about content and amount of detail; the second about the language used.

**5** How helpful do you find the map in the Telegraph? (2 marks)

The map helps you to see the distances involved in the rescue. It does not add much else to the reader's understanding of the story.

Advice

Good answer – the reader's opinion is clearly put.

pages @ 90%

**6** What features of language in both texts do you find typical of newspaper writing? What differences do you notice? (6 marks)

The headlines both use the present tense ('saves'/'flies') to make the story feel as if it's happening now. It makes it more dramatic. Both texts use words like 'twins' and ages to label people ('Ian and Stuart Middle, 27-year-old twin brothers...'). This is typical of newspaper style where as much information as possible is squeezed into a small space.

The opening of each story gives an outline. The rest of each story gives more and more background detail. The Telegraph also uses plenty of eyewitnesses' comments, making it feel factual and well-researched. The Telegraph uses more scientific language – 'nitrogen bubbles can form in the bloodstream' – suggesting an educated audience. The Express, in contrast, focuses more on the emotional drama of the story. Both texts use short paragraphs to keep the story moving.

Advice

This answer identifies some of the key language features well. It would be a better answer, however, if it addressed the two questions separately – a paragraph on the features of newspaper language; then a second paragraph on the differences.

# Autobiography

**Text A**

## My Mam's Death

**1** What ages were the narrator and her younger brother when their mother died? (2 marks)

Narrator: fourteen and a half

Younger brother: two

**2** How does the narrator think her father should have handled the news that her mother was dying? (4 marks)

He told her very abruptly that her mother was going to die. He could have told her the news earlier to prepare her.

B

**3** Why do you think the narrator spends so long getting the house ready for her mother's return from hospital? (4 marks)

She probably wants to make her mother's final days as special as possible. She might also want to show that she is grown-up, responsible enough to start taking charge of the house.

Advice

We aren't given any reasons directly – but the thoughts in this paragraph are convincing and well-expressed.

**4** The writer doesn't include any words spoken by the mother – we hear about her, but we don't hear from her. Why do you think this is? (5 marks)

The real focus of the text is the narrator – her feelings and how she copes with the crisis. I think the narrator is probably so upset by events that she avoids talking directly about her mother. She is trying to come to terms with the experience and so writes about her own feelings in detail.

Advice

Quite a demanding question, this one. To some readers it may seem an odd feature of the text – the narrator is so close to her mother and yet we hardly see them together. The answer here is good and gives a convincing reason for the way the text is written.

**5** Write a paragraph about your response to the text. Do you find it emotional, moving, controlled, neutral? What do you notice about the way the writer has written it? (5 marks)

The text is very moving and emotional, and yet it is written in quite a controlled way. The opening sentence sets the factual tone, and leads into a step-by-step account of what happened. The focus then shifts to the narrator at home preparing for her mother's return. The text becomes more emotional here because it shows how upset the girl is. The description of the period after the mother's death returns to a fairly factual style, chiefly just cataloguing what happened. The vocabulary has an informal feeling – words like 'moped' and 'should've' – which helps us to visualize the teenage girl who has suffered. Towards the end her style feels a bit more formal – 'gradually I picked up the shattered pieces of my torn life'. The style here has an almost poetic feel to it.

Advice

The answer recognizes that the text does not have a simple style. It is a mixture of fact and emotion. It could afford to say more about the way the language works. For example:

The rhythm of the sentences seems to change as the text develops. The opening sentence is very controlled ('When I was...'). By paragraph two it feels closer to speech than writing: 'She came through the operation quite well, which really built up my hopes...') The style here is personal, and almost chatty. It shows the writer's feelings very clearly.

The vocabulary is also personal – 'built up my hopes' rather than 'made me optimistic'. It helps us to understand what the writer is like because she uses everyday words and phrases.

# Autobiography

**Text B**

**Cursed**

**1** How does David Swift's grandmother explain his disability? (2 marks)

She says that it was God punishing him for something he did in an earlier life.

**2** Find a sentence which shows that David Swift blamed himself for being disabled. (2 marks)

Best example: 'I used to wonder what it was I'd done so bad to make me like this.'

**3** What point is the writer making when he talks about cats and dogs? (2 marks)

He looks at the way they are treated – put down when injured – and compares himself to them. He worries that he may be treated in the same way.

**4** Look at the influence on David Swift of his family – in particular his grandmother, mother and father. What effect do their words have upon him? (6 marks)

The comments of David Swift's family have obviously made a deep impression upon him. He writes a lot about their words. The grandmother might actually be trying to help him – by describing his disability as a curse from God which will one day be forgotten. But the problem with this idea is that it places the blame on David himself – it makes him feel that he is the cause. He worries about 'what it was I'd done so bad' in a previous life, and sees his disability as a 'curse'.

His parents hardly seem to care. He is quite forgiving of this, saying 'perhaps [they] were trying to cope with their own lives'. But he is obviously hurt by his treatment – a complete lack of love. His father's attitude seems particularly painful to him – 'My dad made me hard, hard inside'.

The result of all these comments is that David Swift feels isolated and unloved – comparing himself to freaks in a show, and to pets that are about to be killed. It is a sign of the way his family's attitude has shattered his self-esteem.

**Advice**

This is an excellent answer – a crisp account of what each member of the family said, and a final paragraph showing what the effect has been on David Swift. This is a controlled, well-argued response – a model answer. Although it is brief, it covers points very skilfully.

**5** Write a paragraph about your impressions of David Swift's character, supporting your points with close reference to the language of the extract. (8 marks)

David Swift is worried and confused. His self-confidence has been sapped by the comments of his family and when he writes, 'if I'm cursed I ought to be aware of why, didn't I?', the question emphasizes the feelings of confusion he has. He thinks about his parents' attitude and says, 'I don't know' – another sign of his loss of confidence. The later part of the text uses more questions – David wondering if he should be treated like a maimed dog and wondering if God is calling him. The effect of all this has made him seem a loner – someone who chooses to spend his time in graveyards, thinking about death.

We also gain a sense of the writer's bitterness from the text. He uses words like 'punished' and 'cursed' to show how badly treated he has been by members of his family. I think there may also be a hint of self-pity in this – for example, 'He never showed me any sympathy...'. The writer is finding it very hard to come to terms with the way he was treated.

David Swift writes in a style which actually sounds more like spoken text at times – for example, 'I felt as if, well, if...'. The style here is almost chatty. It isn't clear who he is addressing, but it feels as if he may be speaking aloud, perhaps to himself, as a way of coming to terms with his experiences. Quite a few sentences begin with the conjunctions 'and', 'but' and 'so', and this gives the text an informal feel. This makes me think that David Swift may actually be thinking aloud, rather than writing a formal autobiography.

**Advice**

This answer gains marks because it does more than tell us about David Swift's character. It also comments upon his use of language – and makes an interesting point about the text, which is well-supported by quotations.

The answer says nothing about the vocabulary in the extract – which is quite formal. For example, the writer says 'tolerated' when he might have said 'put up with'. This is one reason why the text is difficult to place – is it written or spoken? It has an informal structure with some fairly formal vocabulary.

# Travel writing

Text A

## Hitching through the Yukon

**1** How large is the Yukon territory and what is its population? (2 marks)

It is almost the size of France, with fewer than 25,000 inhabitants.

**2** In the extract, Kate Pullinger meets three different drivers. Write a sentence about each describing who they are. (6 marks)

The first driver is a young woman with a baby, who drives in silence.

The second is a woman in a small Toyota, on her way back from a swimming lesson in Whitehorse.

The third driver is a truck driver whose family have grown up.

Advice

Notice that each sentence here says something about who the driver is and one detail about what she or he is like. It's important that you don't feel the need to copy down all of the information from the text – just select the key details.

**3** At the end of the extract, Kate Pullinger says, 'There is something about this place'. What do you think she means? (4 marks)

She means that the place is very attractive to people – it has a power over them. The woman in the Toyota and the lorry driver have both ended up staying far longer than they had planned. This is a sign of the power of the place.

Advice

This is a good answer because it supports its main point with examples. It doesn't need to be any longer – it answers the question very directly and efficiently.

**4** What do we learn about the Yukon from the extract? (4 marks)

We learn about the vast size of the Yukon and its small population. We are told that the landscape is a combination of mountains, lakes and forests. We also see that towns are far apart, and that there is a large amount of dust. The capital of the Yukon is Whitehorse. The Yukon has a powerful effect on the people who live there – they find it difficult to leave.

Advice

This isn't an easy question because there isn't a lot to say in response. This answer is an efficient one. It just manages to avoid feeling like a list. Try to avoid starting sentences with 'Another thing about the Yukon… Another point…' and so on. Try to vary your sentences, just as you would in more extended writing. Notice how the answer manages to avoid saying 'We learn…' by saying 'We are told…' and 'We see'. This makes the answer seem more varied and interesting.

**5** What impression do you gain of Kate Pullinger from the extract?
(4 marks)

Kate Pullinger seems to have a spirit of adventure – 'the best way to see it… is to hitch–hike' – plus a sense of safety. She discusses early on the possible hazards of hitch–hiking, saying, 'nobody is going to leave anyone standing on the side of the road in the middle of nowhere…'. She clearly thinks about the risks involved, though it might be also that she seems a bit optimistic about the way people would behave. After all, how can she be sure that no one is going to abandon a hitch–hiker at the roadside?

Kate Pullinger has a positive view of people. She doesn't really judge them harshly. She describes the behaviour of the first driver who gives her a lift. The woman has a baby, drives in silence, and smokes a cigar. The writer tells us this but doesn't make any judgement – she doesn't describe her as odd, for example.

She seems to enjoy the company of all the people she meets and just accepts them for what they are. This shows that she is curious about people and outgoing. Similarly her attitude to the landscape is really positive. She describes the dust storms without too much horror – even though one of them makes it almost impossible to see. She is clearly very impressed by the landscape, calling it a 'mountain–lake–forest–river–lover's dream come true'. Again, this shows her positive and generous spirit.

Advice

This looks closely at the text and makes some good points. Occasionally the style feels a bit casual – the word 'really' in the second paragraph, for example, doesn't serve much purpose. More, brief quotations could be used to support ideas.

# Travel writing

Text B

## Travelling through the Sahara

**1** How long does the storm last? (2 marks)

It lasts for three days.

**2** Why are desert storms like this such a threat to the people of the desert? (2 marks)

The storms can kill even experienced herdsmen; also people who make their livelihood through travelling are suddenly unable to travel.

Advice

Either of these points would suffice; the second one is particularly good because it makes a point which isn't directly stated in the text – a sign of a higher-level reading skill.

**3** Why, at the end of the extract, do they need to rush? (2 marks)

They need to catch up with a rival who is heading for the market in Cairo.

B

**4** Michael Asher uses a number of images to create a picture in the reader's mind. Say in your own words what you understand by these images:

'a savage sand-storm punched into us with hammer force' (2 marks)

'sand that streaked across the surface like currents of electricity' (2 marks)

'disappearing into the veil of dust' (2 marks)

'the golden beams of the dwindling sun spread out... like the arms of a giant starfish' (2 marks)

'a savage sand–storm punched into us with hammer force'

'Punched' creates the impression that the storm is human and that it is attacking people on purpose. 'Hammer force' suggests how sharp and painful its effect is.

Advice

Notice how the answer focuses on individual words in the sentence. It is a sign of close reading.

'sand that streaked across the surface like currents of electricity'

The sand moves rapidly across the dunes. It makes a wave formation like electric currents – rather like the image of blue electric waves which are shown in horror films. The image suggests the power and speed of the sand.

Advice

This isn't a very clear response. It doesn't seem to get to the heart of the image. The answer could say:

> The word 'streaked' suggests the speed at which the sand moves. It makes it seem light and unpredictable. The comparison with currents of electricity again suggests the speed of the sand, but also that there is something dangerous about it.

Whether you agree or not with this interpretation of the image, notice how the answer takes specific words and responds to them – 'streaked' … 'currents of electricity'.

> 'disappearing into the veil of dust'
>
> This image suggests the dust is like a thin shroud: as people walk into it they gradually disappear.

Advice

Nicely put.

> 'the golden beams of the dwindling sun spread out... like the arms of a giant starfish'
>
> This makes the sun seem large and attractive, although it is quite an odd image in the context of a desert. Starfish, after all, live in the sea.

Advice

This is the start of an interesting answer. It is good that the writer gives an opinion ('It is quite an odd image'). It probably should say more about what impression we get of the sun – it is 'dwindling' and yet attractive and rather exotic (unusual).

**5** Look more closely at the first paragraph. How does Michael Asher use language to suggest the power of the storm? (6 marks)

> Michael Asher uses vocabulary to suggest the power of the storm – words like 'hammer' and 'savage'. He makes it seem more than just a force of nature. Some of his language makes it feel human, as if the storm is there to hurt people on purpose – for example, 'savage' and 'screamed'.
>
> Michael Asher also shows the storm's power by showing how vulnerable the humans are. He describes their camp as 'a tiny island in the void', showing how small they are in the vast space. He uses words like 'struggle' and 'shivered' to show the effect the storm has on the humans. Even the fire seems to suffer. He says that it 'flickered and trembled'. The storm is fighting everything. All there is for protection is 'blankets' – which sounds quite feeble in the face of the 'hammer force' of the wind. He creates the impression that the storm is winning its battle – the night 'grew colder' and the 'wind more icy'. It is harder and harder for humans to survive. His final image shows how isolated the humans are: 'we shivered at the base of our lone bush'. Just one bush is all they have protecting them.
>
> The language creates a very forceful picture of the power of nature and the vulnerability of humans.

Advice

This is a really good answer, because it highlights the way the writer portrays the human beings, rather than just focusing on the language used to describe the storm. The style of the answer could be cleaned up a bit: it repeats the word 'shows'/'showing', and in the last sentence of the second paragraph, the word 'fighting' feels a bit weak. 'Conquering' or even 'bullying' might have been more effective choices.

The answer looks systematically at the whole paragraph and then gives a concluding sentence – 'The language creates a very forceful picture of the power of nature and the vulnerability of humans.' This is good because it draws the answer to a close and emphasizes that the student has answered the question very directly.

# Campaigning advertisements

Text A

## The Samaritans campaign ad

1 Look again at the slogan at the foot of the advertisement: 'We'll go through it with you'. Which of the statements below do you think best describes what the slogan means?

'We will explain it all clearly to you.'

'We know about suffering.'

'We will support you.'

'We're only a phone call away.' (1 mark)

'We will support you' is the best choice because the slogan is emphasizing that the Samaritans will be there with the person who is suffering.

2 Say in your own words what the main heading means: 'Sometimes it's easier to talk to someone you don't like'. (3 marks)

'At times you need to talk to someone whom you do not know well.'

3 The advertisement gives reasons why someone may not want to discuss a problem with a close friend or a member of the family. What are they? (4 marks)

One reason is that a close friend may not be reliable. She or he might 'end up telling the world'. It may be too embarrassing to tell a member of the family. It can be hard to talk to people we are really close to because it involves showing our weaknesses. Sometimes the problem is the relationship – so you wouldn't want to discuss it with the person involved.

Advice

This is a good answer because it makes the points crisply and clearly, but in the writer's own words.

4 How well does the layout of the advertisement add to its effect? (6 marks)

The layout centres on a large image of a young woman who appears to be smiling. The question inside the photograph box suggests that this is an image of a girlfriend. This tells us something about the target audience of the advertisement – it seems to be aimed at young men. The main slogan, to the left of the photograph, also suggests this. It says, 'Sometimes it's easier to talk to someone you don't like', which seems to be hinting at the idea of men finding it difficult to talk to people.

Underneath the photograph there are two columns of text. These are presented in short paragraphs as a way of keeping us reading. The name of the charity at the bottom is printed in a straightforward style, with the slogan, 'We'll go through it with you' in a black box for emphasis.

Overall the advertisement catches our attention with the large image of the girlfriend and the surprise of the slogan about talking to 'someone you don't like'. This is very effective – the image and words seem to clash, making us read the text below.

Advice

This answer addresses the main points of layout well. The point about the slogan on the left is not, strictly speaking, a layout point: it is to do with the way the advertisement uses language. But it does help to explain the image chosen and therefore fits with the rest of the answer. The answer identifies the way the advertisement works, and then (at the end) talks about how effective it is. This is good – it shows that the student has the ability to make a judgement about the layout.

**5** How does the language of the advertisement help us to feel that the Samaritans are on our side? (6 marks)

The advertisement has a very reassuring tone. It makes it feel natural that talking to people can be difficult. For example, 'sometimes we don't want to expose our weaknesses to those who fancy us'. The use of the word 'fancy' here is informal, and makes it feel as if the advertisement is speaking to a young audience. It isn't stuffy at all.

The advertisement uses 'you' and 'we' quite a lot. This makes it feel as if there is a link between the Samaritans and the reader – as if they understand us – for example: 'We're more discreet than your best mate'. It's almost as if they know us because of the way they talk about 'your best mate'.

The language feels different at one point. When it says 'we're also non-judgemental, unshockable and extremely experienced', this seems much more formal than the earlier vocabulary. I think the effect is to make us feel that the Samaritans are reliable. The words are formal but also reassuring. They contrast with the earlier words like 'fancy' and 'best mate', and therefore make us feel that the Samaritans are detached from problems and therefore good to turn to.

Advice

Although this answer sometimes feels a bit clumsy (for example, the last sentence of the second paragraph), it contains some perceptive points about language. Students often avoid looking at language in detail and, as a result, they can miss out on the top marks. This answer shows the reader focusing quite specifically on the words, and quoting them to support points made. The final point, about the formal language ('non-judgemental', etc.), is a very high-level response. It shows the student spotting an important language feature and trying to explain its effect.

# Campaigning advertisements

Text B

## Sight Savers campaign ad

**1** Based on the advertisement, write down two facts about trachoma. (2 marks)

Some possibilities:

- It causes your eyes to itch.
- It burns into the eyelid, leaving a scar.
- It keeps recurring.
- It harms your eyelashes and eyelids.
- It makes you go blind.
- It is cured with Tetracycline.

**2** What can be used to treat trachoma quickly and effectively? (2 marks)

Tetracycline ointment can be used.

**3** Comment on the main image and slogan ('Blinking Hell'). Discuss what you think the advertisers hope to achieve through them. Do you think they work? (4 marks)

The main image shows a pair of eyes shining brightly, with barbed wire eyelashes above and below them. The image is very eye-catching and suggests the pain which sufferers of trachoma feel. The text below talks about the burning feeling which the disease causes – the image of the barbed wire is a powerful way of making us imagine what it might feel like.

The slogan is a play on words. Blinking is sometimes used as a mild curse – 'stop the blinking noise' and 'blinking hell'. Here the 'hell' part is referring to the pain of the blinking: in other words blinking will feel as painful as hell.

Together, the image and slogan are quite powerful. The advertisers want us to pause and read the advertisement, and it probably achieves this.

Advice

This is a good, systematic answer – a paragraph on the image and another on the slogan. Both are explained well. The last paragraph is an evaluation of what the advertisers are trying to achieve. The answer doesn't seem to think that the advertisement is fully successful – it says 'probably' – and perhaps this could be made clearer: why doesn't the advertisement fully achieve its aim?

**4** How does the advertisement use language to make the reader feel involved? (6 marks)

The first sentence leaves us feeling unsure of what is happening. It is as if we are joining the middle of a conversation and it is not clear what the pronoun 'it' is referring to. This is a good way of drawing us quickly into the text: it makes us keen to read on to find out what is 'not too bad'.

The text then goes on to describe the process of the disease. It takes us, step by step, through the way trachoma develops. The language is fairly informal – 'it's' and 'don't' instead of the more formal versions of these words – and this helps to hold our interest. The language creates a feeling of how simple the process is: 'And that's all it takes to spread trachoma'. I think that this makes us realize how difficult it must be to avoid the disease. It makes us see the people who get it as helpless victims.

The really big shift in language is from 'they' to 'you' – as in 'You only notice there's something wrong...' Suddenly the text has changed. Instead of us being outside looking in on the disease, we are part of the scene, looking at a child suffering. This is a really powerful device which makes us feel very involved in the text.

The later part of the advertisement has its effect by showing us how easy the suffering would be to avoid. It says that this is the 'utterly horrifying thing' and goes on to show how cheap a cure can be. The final section uses figures to persuade us how easy it would be for us to help, and how different sums of money could have a different effect. To encourage us to make a contribution the advertisment uses a question: 'Wouldn't you pay a hundred or a thousand times that if it were your eyes at stake?' Having shown us how little we need to contribute, the writer then makes us think about our own values and hints that if we don't pay we would be being selfish. It is an effective method for persuading us.

**Advice** You can sense how good this answer is. Look at the very clear and controlled response to the question; the use of short quotations to support points; the sensitivity to the way the tone of the text changes. This is the kind of answer at GCSE to aim for!

**5** The text uses phrases like 'agonisingly slowly', 'utterly horrifying', 'totally unnecessary'. Discussing each of these examples, decide what effect they have. (6 marks)

'Agonisingly slowly': the language here creates a sense of the sheer pain the victims of trachoma feel. The adverb 'agonisingly' refers to the pain and emphasizes how slowly it all happens. The word is a good choice because it is a long word which slows the text down. I mean by this that it sort of creates the effect of slow pain.

'Utterly horrifying': this phrase uses the word 'horrifying' to suggest how terrible the suffering of the victims is. It adds the adverb 'utterly' to reinforce this – to make it even more extreme. The phrase seems to suggest that it is as horrifying as it is possible to be – extreme language to show extreme pain.

'Totally unnecessary': this phrase also uses an adverb to emphasize something. It is making the point that the pain suffered by victims of trachoma is not necessary because it can easily be cured. Instead of just describing this as 'unnecessary' it emphasizes how unnecessary it is by using the word 'totally'.

**Advice** This isn't an easy question because it is very focused on some small examples of language. The answer takes the right approach: writing the phrases down and then writing a short paragraph analysing each one. The answers successfully explore each phrase. It is impressive to see the writer trying very hard to explain points that are difficult to express – as in the last sentence of the first paragraph.

# Biography

## Text A

### Sally Gunnell biography

**1** Why did the 400 metre race in Barcelona have to be restarted? (2 marks)

The runner in Lane 8 made a false start.

**2** Write down a sentence from the biography which shows that Sally Gunnell is very determined. (2 marks)

There are two main examples:

'She thought, "You're ahead, so go for it!"'

'As usual, she put everything except the race out of her mind.'

(B)

**3** How can you tell that the writer of the biography admires Sally Gunnell? (4 marks)

The biographer calls her 'Sally'. This makes her sound as if she likes her. If she called her 'Gunnell' all the time it would sound much more formal and impersonal. The writer also shows us how much self-discipline Sally Gunnell has – for example, 'Sally never takes any medicines for colds or headaches'. It sounds as if the writer really admires Sally Gunnell's control. She also makes Sally Gunnell feel very human – for example by telling us that 'she also loves going to McDonalds for a hamburger and she likes chips and chocolate'. In a way this shows us the human side of Sally Gunnell and shows that the writer admires the kind of person she is.

**Advice**

This is quite a good answer. Each point is well-supported by a quotation, and the quotations are well chosen. The first point, about Sally Gunnell's name, is the best point and the answer explains it well, showing what the effect would be if the writer called her 'Gunnell' all the time.

The student does repeat the word 'admires', however. It would be better to find a different word the second time – 'respects', for example.

**4** How well does the writer help us to learn what Sally Gunnell is really like? (6 marks)

The writer calls Sally Gunnell by her first name, helping us to feel that we know her. She also shows us what Sally Gunnell is thinking: 'She thought, "You're ahead, so go for it!".' It is difficult to know how the writer could know what is actually in Sally Gunnell's mind, but it does help us to feel that we know her. The writer gives us information about Sally Gunnell's private feelings – her love of hamburgers and chocolate. If we only had descriptions of her in races, she would not feel so human. The writer also shows us how Sally deals with colds, and how disappointed she feels when things don't go right. At Stuttgart Sally Gunnell says to herself, 'I made a mistake, so I know I can run faster than that.' This also increases her human qualities.

Advice

This answer is fine but it doesn't go far enough. It couldn't get full marks, however good it is, because it hasn't addressed the second part of the question about how successful the writer is ('How well does the writer help us to learn what Sally Gunnell is really like?').

It needs a final comment like:

The writer shows us some of the human qualities of Sally Gunnell rather than just concentrating on her athletic abilities. To feel we really know Sally Gunnell we would need to know more about her - her background, how she got involved in running, her hopes and fears - but as a starting-point the text is quite successful in showing what she is really like.

Advice

This suddenly improves the whole answer – partly because it addresses the question fully and partly because the writer gives a well thought-out opinion.

**5** Look at the language of the text. How can you tell that it is written for a young audience? (6 marks)

The text describes the events at Barcelona as if it was the beginning of a made-up story: 'It was a hot August day in Barcelona'. This gives it a young feel. The writer also makes some points which feel very obvious - for example, 'The first athlete to cross the finishing line would win the gold medal'. Most people would know this, unless they were very young.

The text uses lots of short, simple sentences, as in 'she had started too soon'. This gives the description a simple and direct feel. There is nothing complicated here. When it stops using narrative and describes instead what athletes have to eat, the style is still very straightforward. We might expect some technical detail about what athletes must and mustn't eat. The writer uses 'vitamins, 'minerals', and 'zinc', but nothing more complicated.

The vocabulary in general is very easy to follow - for example, the writer says 'The rules about drug taking are very tough'. Instead of 'tough' she might have said 'stringent' or 'demanding', if the text had been aimed at an older audience.

Advice

This is quite a technical answer. It starts by looking at the tone of the text ('as if it was the beginning of a made-up story…'). Then it analyses sentence length ('short, simple sentences…'). Then it describes the vocabulary ('very easy to follow'). The structure of this answer is very clear and each point is supported by a quotation. It is a very good response.

# Biography

## Text B

### The Detective

**1** Why might it seem 'a little weird' that George Barrett kisses his four sons goodnight each evening? (2 marks)

Two of his sons are seventeen and nineteen. They might seem a little grown-up to be kissed goodnight.

**2** How can you tell that George Barrett does not respect the criminals he is after? (2 marks)

He describes them using terms like 'these animals' and 'germs'. He calls Broadway 'the sewer'.

Advice

This answer probably gives slightly more detail than is needed, but it is very clearly and directly stated.

**3** The text gives a clear picture of George Barrett. Write a paragraph showing what he is like – his character, his background, his attitude. Is there anything to admire about him? (6 marks)

Our first impression is of a caring man. He is shown kissing his family goodnight. Then we get a description of him – for example, 'his eyes, cold as gun-metal...'. All of the description shows his toughness – for example, 'his jaw is hard and square as a brick'. The toughness of his appearance matches the toughness of his character.

The writer then gives a flashback to George Barrett's earlier life. He shows the brutal experiences of his childhood, and this shows how George Barrett learnt about violence: 'I do what has to be done'. This shows that he has become immune to the violence, seeing it as part of the job.

George Barrett is a successful detective who has been promoted because of his good work. Although he is ruthless, he is doing a good job in fighting crime. As the writer says at the start about law enforcement: 'To others he is all that can save it'. I think the fact that we see his sensitive side and his background makes us admire the job he does and the way he does it.

Advice

This is a first-rate answer. It clearly organizes the main points about George Barrett's character, supporting them with quotations, and it addresses the second part of the question: whether there is anything to admire in him. Notice in particular how short quotations can be embedded in your answer, making it more fluent to read, and less disjointed.

**4** How does the writer use language to create the atmosphere of downtown New York? (5 marks)

The writer uses descriptive visual language – 'the flashing neon fireball of Times Square'. His language makes the place seem fascinating and yet unpleasant, partly because of the dramatic, negative words used, such as 'sewer' and 'germs'. This shows us how Barrett views the scene and it has the feeling of a jungle. The writer uses words like 'prowling' and 'hunting' to make it all feel wild and dangerous.

The writer lists other details, moving through them quickly. He doesn't describe any of the criminals in detail. He just creates an impression of the prostitutes, pimps and car boosters. He describes the last group in more detail, but always shows them as a group. We never get a picture of the individuals involved in the crime. For this reason, the criminals feel impersonal and, again, animal-like, carefully calculating their next move and attack.

As a result, we can sense how exciting the scene is, as well as how dangerous.

He describes the different types of people on the street, including prostitutes who sit with 'velvet chairs and phony flowers'. This detail hints at the fact that they try to look high class – 'velvet' – but are actually quite cheap – 'phony flowers'.

The writer uses quite a lot of lists to show the variety of the scene. It has a lively, bustling feel because of phrases like this: 'vicious cousins, the A&R men, assault and robbery specialists, muggers'. The streets are teeming with life, and the lists emphasize this impression.

Advice

This is a good answer. It focuses well on the language, noting vocabulary points and grammatical structures (e.g. use of lists). Another grammar point is the fairly long sentences used by the writer – again, these hint at a place that is barely in control. Short, controlled sentences would probably create a very different effect.

**5** Some readers feel that the text glorifies violence. Others think James Mills shows life as it really is. Comment on the portrayal of violence in the extract. (5 marks)

The text hints that New York is a very violent place but it avoids showing direct examples. The writer says that people are hurt and attacked, but he doesn't describe what happens in any detail. The language of the text uses fairly aggressive vocabulary – for example, 'if I have to, I'll use my gun' and describing people as 'animals', the streets as 'the sewer'. This shows us what a hardened cop George Barrett is, and what a tough world New York streets can be. I'm not sure that it glorifies violence, though – instead, it seems to show what life is like for people there.

Also, the writer shows the effects of violence. George Barrett seems to join the police force as a result of the violence in his childhood. He wants to do something about it. This isn't glorifying the violence. It is showing how it leads to someone wanting to fight crime and so the message is that crime and violence are wrong.

Advice

This is fine, but it would have been clearer in two sections. The first would look at the evidence that the text is glorifying violence ('I… tattooed them into the ground with the bottles…'); and then evidence that it all has a purpose – to show us that violence is wrong.

# Information texts

**Text A**

**'Exercise and Fitness' information text**

**1** Look at the list of activities printed on page 85 and answer the questions. Name an activity which is:

**a** especially good for suppleness
**b** especially good for sociability
**c** very good for strength, stamina and sociability
**d** poor for strength and stamina
**e** best overall for all categories (5 marks)

Advice

Notice that there is one mark for each answer. Since the question asks you simply to name an activity, you can just write down one word as an answer. You don't need to write 'An activity which is good for stamina is…'. But if you are ever in doubt about this, write a full sentence.

a) especially good for suppleness

Name one from: dancing, fencing, gymnastics, ice hockey, judo/karate, skating, skiing, squash, swimming

b) especially good for sociability

Again, name one from: baseball, dancing, rowing, downhill skiing

c) very good for strength, stamina and sociability

rowing

This is the only activity which has ★★★ for each category.

d) poor for strength and stamina

billiards/darts

These activities don't score any points for these features.

e) best overall for all categories

dancing and swimming

These two activities gain the highest scores overall.

**2** Why is a mixture of activities a good idea? (2 marks)

A mixture will prevent you from getting bored after a few weeks.

**3** Name one disadvantage of sport. (2 marks)

You can get injured quite easily.

**4** Write a paragraph recommending suitable activities to someone who can't see the point of exercise. (5 marks)

*You might not think exercise is for you – but think again! There are all kinds of activities which will help to keep you in shape whilst also letting you meet new friends. And they don't have to be expensive. Take swimming. It's one of the most effective ways of building your suppleness, strength and stamina – yet it's also one of the most economical activities available. It does more for your strength than playing squash. So take another look at exercise. It will do you good and help you feel better about yourself.*

Advice

This has a good, lively tone. It feels like part of a leaflet promoting sport. The writer achieves an enthusiastic tone by addressing the reader very directly ('you') and using short, snappy sentences ('Take swimming.'). It is a neatly constructed paragraph – it starts by encouraging readers to take more exercise; then suggests a specific example; and concludes by urging them again to take more exercise.

**5** Are there any clues in the language that this information text might have been written for a young audience? (6 marks)

*Whilst at some points this text feels very much as if it were written for a young audience, there are points when it is not so clear-cut. The opening sentence is direct and easily understandable by all readers. But the second sentence uses more complex vocabulary, such as 'conceivable' and 'competitive'. These are not words that hint at a younger age group. The writer addresses the audience quite directly, with expressions like, 'You are going to spend quite a lot of time carrying out your exercise...' but this does not really suggest what age the reader might be.*

*My impression overall is that the text is written for a general audience which isn't old or young. Instead it is written for readers who are simply interested in sport. The main evidence for this is that the vocabulary is quite high-level, whilst the sentences are fairly straightforward and not complex.*

Advice

This is a fair answer to a tricky question. The text – as the answer says – does not contain a clear sense of audience. The answer is good because it focuses clearly on the language of the text – the sentences and the vocabulary.

# Information texts

Text B

## 'Aircraft Technology' information text

A

**1** When did long-distance flights by air begin to be made? (2 marks)

They began soon after the end of the First World War.

**2** Name one of the first modern airliners. (2 marks)

One of the first modern airliners was the Douglas DC-2.

Advice

You might mention instead the Boeing 247.

This is an example of an answer where a full sentence answer may not be necessary. You could probably just write the name of the aircraft. As ever, if in doubt, write it out in full, as above.

**3** Why is it important that an aircraft should carry as many passengers as possible? (2 marks)

Carrying as many passengers as possible makes the aircraft more profitable: the more people who pay to fly on the plane, the more money the company can make.

B

**4** What have been the main stages in the development of aircraft from the First World War to the present day? Write your answer as a list of numbered points. (5 marks)

1 At the end of the First World War, two-winged aeroplanes were first used to carry passengers.
2 In the mid-1930s the first all-metal low-wing monoplanes were built, proving faster and more economical than earlier aircraft.
3 After the Second World War the first turbojet engine was designed. After early problems it was redesigned in 1958 and has since formed the basis of modern aircraft.
4 In 1969 wide-bodied aircraft were introduced.
5 Later developments include the computerized cockpit, as in the Boeing 747-400.

Advice

This answer clearly identifies the main stages required by the question. It is specific without giving too much detail.

**5** Look at the panel about supersonic flight. Draw a diagram and label it to show readers how supersonic flight works. Then write about how clear you found the information to follow. (4 marks)

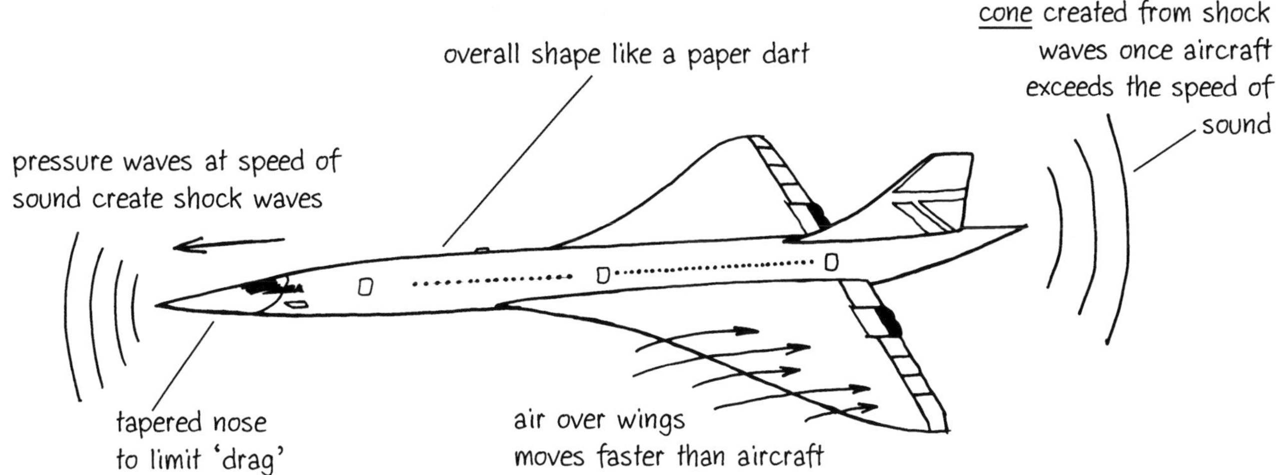


I felt that I understood most of the description, but it was hard to translate the words into a diagram. I used labels to try to show what I meant. There were a few terms in the text, such as 'drag' and 'turbulent', which could perhaps have been put more simply.

Advice

This illustration captures the main details of the text, and the labels make up for the student's lack of skill in drawing. The comment about how easy the text was to follow is good. The student is right to comment on certain technical words. She might have gone further and talked about the problem of knowing how much detail to put onto the diagram – for example, should the sonic boom be drawn? A student who says in an answer, 'I decided not to include this because…' would show that the detail wasn't just left out because she didn't understand it. In other words, try to keep the examiner fully informed about your reasons for doing things.

**6** Comment on the language of the extract. How clear is it? How well does it take complicated ideas and present them simply? How could the extract be improved? (5 marks)

The text contains a lot of information. It gives plenty of specific information about dates and types of aeroplane. The style the writer uses is quite a direct one. The sentences feel well-controlled and informative – as in the first paragraph. The vocabulary is mostly straightforward, though the writer could explain technical terms like monoplanes (he does explain biplanes, earlier, by saying 'two-winged aeroplanes…').

The text could be improved by adding subheadings to paragraphs. This would make the development of aircraft easier to follow. Some possible subheadings include: 'After the First World War', 'The Second World War', 'Recent Years'. These would help the reader to see the progress of aircraft more clearly.

I don't think the style of writing could be much improved.

Advice

This is a clear and well-organized response. It comments on the text quite closely (though it could do with an example of well-controlled and informative sentences: for example, 'Smaller airliners, such as the Boeing 757 and 767, are also equipped with digital cockpits', or 'Amongst the latest airliners is the wide-bodied Boeing 747-400.' It makes a useful point about how the text might be improved. It is well expressed.

# Advertorials

Text A

## Norwich Union Direct advertorial

**1** How has Louise White saved £250? (2 marks)

She has saved the money by buying her car insurance from Norwich Union Direct.

**2** In what ways does this advertising feature look like a newspaper article? (4 marks)

You might say:

It uses a headline ('Aisle save £250 on car cover') and strapline ('Boost for bride Lou').
The headline uses a play on words ('aisle' rather than 'I'll').
The format includes a photograph.
The text is produced in columns with short paragraphs.
It also uses a subheading ('Helpful') to feel like a real newspaper.

Advice

You should write your answer in paragraph form, rather than as a list of points. The suggested answer above should pick up four marks because it makes five points. However, the second point – about the wordplay in the headline – is a bit unnecessary here. The question asks about how the text *looks* like a newspaper article – 'aisle'/'I'll' is actually not related to layout, but it is to do with meaning. It would probably be better left out of this answer.

**3** Read the first five paragraphs. At what point do you think a reader would realize that the text was an advertisement feature? Explain your answer. (4 marks)

The first paragraph feels like the beginning of a real newspaper article. It is the second paragraph which makes us start to wonder. The reference to 'Norwich Union Direct' takes us by surprise. We might expect the writer to say 'her insurance company', but this is so much more specific. The fifth paragraph feels much more like an advertisement because it is so obviously presenting a positive view of the company: 'Norwich Union Direct came up with the answer to her problems'.

Advice

This is a good answer. It is well supported by quotations and it makes its points clearly.

**4** Look at the right-hand column headlined 'End Guy Fawkes Thieves'. Why do you think this feature has been included? (4 marks)

This column feels more like advice to the reader, rather than a story about someone's experiences. It aims to make readers realize how much at risk they are from burglary, so that they might choose Norwich Union Direct home insurance. It also gives useful hints, to encourage readers to see Norwich

Union Direct as experts who can be relied upon. The text isn't just a list of suggestions and advice. It also feels closer to an advertisement by the end, because it says quite directly 'Call free on...'

Advice

This answer picks up on the different tone of this text from the main story. What is particularly impressive is that the answer shows that the writer has thought about the reasons for this column of text. It is also a good answer because it spots a change of purpose within the text – from advice to straight advertising at the end.

Notice how the student's style could be improved. The phrase 'It also' is repeated several times and feels clumsy. A better answer might say 'Another reason that...'; 'A further possibility is...', or use other phrases which create variety.

**5** The advertorial 'Aisle Save £250...' certainly *looks* like a newspaper article. Does it also read like one? Write a paragraph or more discussing the style of the text – ways in which it does feel like a newspaper article and ways in which it doesn't. (6 marks)

The headline is similar to a real newspaper article's headline. It uses a fairly corny pun, 'Aisle' instead of 'I'll', which is something that tabloid newspapers quite often do. The strapline – 'Boost for Bride Lou' – also makes this feel like a real newspaper story, for two reasons. First, it shortens the subject's name – from Louise to Lou. Newspapers often do this (Gazza, Hezze, Jacko). It also uses repetition of sounds – <u>b</u>oost and <u>b</u>ride.

The caption under the photograph uses a typical newspaper technique, though I don't think it works. 'Steer–ly in love' rather than 'clearly' or 'really' confused me at first and I couldn't get the joke.

To me the story doesn't really read like a real newspaper story because it doesn't describe anything dramatic. Newspaper stories are usually about events which took place the day before and which contained some special feature – drama or surprise or comedy. This story is all about someone who takes out car insurance. It therefore feels rather flat and unexciting.

Advice

This answer pays good attention to the language of the text. The writer clearly knows about newspaper styles and is able to comment on them knowledgeably. The writer picks up on newspaper techniques like alliteration – repeating first sounds in words. What is also impressive is the way the answer is quite critical of the advertorial, saying which parts work and don't work. This gives the examiner the feeling that this is someone with opinions as well as knowledge.

The writer could have also mentioned that an author's name is given – unusual in advertising; and could have noted the change in style within the text: the last five paragraphs of the article are in a different style to that of the opening 'story'.

# Advertorials

Text B

## Memory and Concentration Studies advertorial

**1** In what ways does this text look like a newspaper article? (4 marks)

You might mention:

- use of headline
- photograph
- columns
- sub-headings.

Advice

Remember to write your answer as a paragraph rather than a list of bullet points.

**2** What do you think the advertisement means in the final paragraph when it says 'No obligation'? (2 marks)

It means that you will not be expected to buy the product.

**3** Name three of the benefits of learning the memory technique, according to the advertorial. (3 marks)

You would not forget appointments. You could learn faster. You could memorize whole books. You could do better in exams. You could be more confident at parties.

Advice

Three points are available, so you just need to list three benefits.

**4** What can you tell from the advertorial about who it is aimed at? (5 marks)

The advertorial is specifically aimed at readers of The Independent. You can tell this from the final paragraph. It presents a picture of people who are a bit nervous about their abilities, possibly lacking confidence in themselves. The first paragraph lists people in different roles; the second suggests people who are being held back in their role because their memory lets them down – people who are 'embarrassed'; others who 'lose business, academic and social opportunities.' The list of benefits shows what a wide range of people the advertorial is aimed at – people in a variety of roles who use their memories for different purposes.

Whilst it is aimed at all these people of different backgrounds, what they all have in common is a lack of confidence in their use of memory. This is what the advertorial chiefly addresses.

However, the advertisement feels sexist. It features the image of a man, and lists 'businessmen, professional men, salesmen', and 'housewives'. This list implies that men have important jobs and women don't.

Advice

This answer is fine, but it might say more about the intellect of readers. The intended audience is an intelligent one. They are expected to read a broadsheet newspaper (*The Independent*) and to be people whose careers may involve business or whose private lives might involve being witty at parties and dinners. There is little to hint at the likely age of the intended audience.

**5** How successful do you think the advertorial is? (6 marks)

Advice

Say what you think, but try to support responses with direct quotations. Here are some of the kinds of points you might consider:

**Positive**

- The question in the headline grabs attention.
- The advertorial does address a common worry – and shows how people might make progress.
- It makes the memory technique sound very simple and powerful.

**Negative**

- It gives very little detail about the technique.
- The photograph doesn't really add to the effect – it seems a bit of a waste of space.
- The first two paragraphs don't really grab our attention – I wouldn't want to read on.

# Comparison by theme

## Magazine article and information text

(A)

**1** Write down one fact from the first text. (2 marks)

Advice

There are plenty to choose from. They include:

Adam Woodyatt is 28.
He joined the cast of 'EastEnders' at 16.
He got his present PC in 1991.
Adam Woodyatt uses email to send some letters.

All of these are, as far as we can tell, facts rather than opinions. Notice that you only need to give one to gain two marks.

**2** Write down one fact from the second text. (2 marks)

Some possibilities:

30 million people have so far joined the Internet.
Electronic mail is usually faster and cheaper than telephone or ordinary mail.
You can shop on the Internet.

**3** Write down one opinion from the first text. (2 marks)

Advice

This is trickier. You need to look out for statements which are telling you about what the writer thinks or feels rather than what is factual. Some possibilities:

Adam Woodyatt was in the last generation not to do computer studies at school.
The Internet is quite addictive.
There is no limit to what you can get on the Internet.
If people knew he was Ian Beale, he would gets lots of email.

**4** Write down one opinion from the second text. (2 marks)

Once you're connected you'll find there's plenty to do…
Finding your way around the Web is easy.
It's amazing what you can find when surfing.

(B)

**5** How do the two texts reassure someone that using a computer is straightforward and not frightening? (6 marks)

Text A shows us someone who didn't know much about computers becoming confident. Adam Woodyatt says that as a child 'I didn't have a clue what I was doing'. His style is quite informal, and this helps readers to feel that computers are not just for technical whizz-kids. For example, he says 'didn't have a clue' rather than something more formal like 'didn't know' or 'didn't understand'. Adam Woodyatt sometimes addresses the reader directly – 'You just point the mouse to what you want...' – and this makes us feel more involved, as if he is reassuring us that we can also use computers.

Text B also uses fairly informal language: 'Once you're connected you'll find there's plenty to do...'. The language here is like conversation in a way: 'you'll' and 'there's' are the kinds of words we might expect in everyday speech. Like Adam Woodyatt's article, text B makes the reader feel involved. For example, it says: 'you don't have to worry about the complexities of how computers communicate with each other – you just point and click on your PC'. This is really similar to Adam Woodyatt's advice and makes using a computer seem easy. The way the article lists all the different things you can do – shopping, making contacts and so on – also reassures the reader because it shows that computers are about real purposes rather than just clever technical features.

Advice

This answer contains good points but is a bit haphazard. It needs a more systematic structure. It might be better in four paragraphs – the first about vocabulary in text A; the second about vocabulary in text B; the third about the ideas in text A; the fourth about the ideas in text B... or something like that. This would help the reader to feel clearer about what the writer is saying.

**6** The two texts belong to different genres (types of writing). What do you notice about the language of text A which is typical of personal writing, and what do you notice about the language of text B which makes it seem typical of an information text? (6 marks)

Text A has one main feature of personal writing – use of the pronoun 'I'. It uses informal vocabulary – such as 'reckon' for 'think' or 'believe'. The organization of the text is chronological – it starts with the writer as a child and works up to the present day.

Text B uses more technical terms – like 'Getting on-line' and 'download software'. But it isn't trying to confuse us. Instead its style shows us that technical terms can have a real purpose. The use of bullet points is something we expect in a leaflet but probably not in an autobiography: they allow the writer to give short chunks of information which the reader can take in quickly. The information text has a clear feeling of advising readers: 'Finding your way around the web is easy...'. It gives information and also leads readers into the Internet.

Advice

This is an observant response, but rather short. The writer could have gained more marks by noting the points in the advice box following the questions. These bring in other aspects not mentioned here – for example:

Look at what we learn about the writer. Look at the way the writer sometimes uses exclamation marks at the ends of sentences to give them an informal style.
Look at how technical information is made simple.
Look out for words like 'amazing' and 'easy'. What effect do they have?
Look at the layout features of the text – how are these typical of information texts?

An answer using some of these points might look like this:

Text A feels like a piece of personal writing. It includes Adam Woodyatt's name and his picture. He writes about himself using the first person pronoun 'I' and describes who he is: 'I'm 28 and I reckon...'. Text B, in contrast, is much more impersonal. We don't learn who the writer is, even though the heading hints that it might be personal because it says 'Why do I need the Internet?'

Text A feels informal because of some of the vocabulary. Words like 'reckon' are used, rather than a more formal term like 'think' or 'believe'. The sentences feel as if they are being spoken aloud, rather than written: 'Then there was the Great Leap Forward...'. This has a chatty feeling to it. Text B is also quite informal, but it feels like a set of instructions, or advice, rather than a personal account. Many of the sentences begin with a main verb: 'Make... Go... Use...' We are being told here what we should do – the tone is more direct and formal than text A.

Text A uses hardly any technical terms. Its whole point is to show how user-friendly computers can be. Statistics like 'the modern computer has more processing power than the one that sent the first spacecraft to the moon' are designed to show us the power of computers, and how far they have developed – and it does this without using technical jargon.

Text B also avoids technical language, but its aim is to help us understand what some terms – like 'World Wide Web' – mean. Its purpose is to explain and therefore it has a different tone: 'often written as WWW and called "the Web".' This feels like a teacher's voice, rather than an autobiography.

Words like 'amazing' and 'easy' are intended to make us realize that computers are powerful and creative, but that they don't have to be complicated or frightening to use.

The layout of text A draws us in by giving the image of an actor who will be known to millions of television viewers. It illustrates the point that you don't have to be a computer expert to use them. The article is structured in medium length paragraphs.

Text B uses the features of information texts to present information – headings, questions, and bullet-points. These are designed to make information easy to locate and read.

# Letters

## Text A

### Wartime letter

**1** Even before you read this text in detail, you can see that it is a letter. Write down three clues that show you. (3 marks)

Advice

You might mention:

- address at the top
- date
- the way the reader is addressed ('Darling Mummy…'): you wouldn't start an assignment like this
- the way the writer concludes: 'Lots of love & kisses Lucia'

Remember: there are three marks available. You should aim to make three different points. Write them all in one paragraph. Your answer will probably start:

The first clue that this is a letter is…

**2** What is the writer finding almost unbearable? (3 marks)

She is very upset by the way some members of the platoon speak about her and her friends.

**3** How would you describe the tone of the letter – is it cheerful, upset, angry, worried? Choose a word (either your own or one of these) which best describes the tone and write a sentence supporting your choice. (4 marks)

Advice

You could choose one of the words suggested – cheerful, upset, angry, worried – or a word of your own. The way to gain marks in this question is to write a sentence which explains your choice. Probably three of the four marks will come from your supporting sentence. Here's a sample:

Desperate

The tone of the letter is desperate. The writer tries to create a brave face, but her anxiety is obvious: 'really it isn't much fun, especially as you know I hate having nasty things said about me'.

**4** What picture do you gain of the writer from her letter? Write a paragraph about her personality. (5 marks)

The writer seems to come from a higher social class. She refers to her mother as 'Darling Mummy' and is called 'Lucia'. She describes her friends as 'sweet'. The language hints at someone from a wealthy background. The way the writer reacts to the language of the members of the platoon also shows that she is not comfortable with ordinary people. I get a strong impression of someone who is unhappy because she doesn't really fit in.

Advice

This is a convincing answer – that is, it expresses clearly its ideas and they seem to fit in with the text. We don't learn much from the answer about what the writer herself is like. It focuses quite a lot on her social class, and could probably say more about relationships with others. For example:

- The term 'Mummy' suggests a close relationship with her mother.
- She worries about relationships with some of the others – complaining of their 'filthy remarks'. This shows that she has different standards and expectations from them.
- She seems to get on well with the NCOs, describing them as 'very sweet and human'.
- Her worries about her own future as an NCO suggest she lacks confidence.

**5** How can you tell from the language that this is an informal letter – written from one person to someone she knows well? (5 marks)

The date is written in a casual way – as if this is a note rather than a formal letter. The writer begins and ends her letter in a very informal way – in particular, 'Lots of love and kisses' is the way we would conclude a note to someone we know well. The language is quite informal, too: 'I'm' rather than 'I am'; '&' rather than 'and'; 'haven't' rather than 'have not'; plus some vocabulary which is quite chatty – 'fed up', 'really isn't much fun'.

Advice

Though brief, this answer shows good attention to detail. It would gain marks because each sentence makes a relevant point. The writer uses the advice points after the question to structure an answer and, as a result, does well. One thing would improve the answer: it needs some alternative words to 'informal' to make it less repetitive. 'Colloquial' is a useful word in this context. Colloquial language is language that is chatty and informal.

# Letters

Text B

## Save the Children letter

A

**1** In what ways does the text look like a letter? (2 marks)

Advice

There are two marks here, so play safe and try to make two points. Some possibilities:

- The main text begins 'Dear Friend', making it look like a letter.
- It ends 'Yours sincerely'.
- It has a signature at the end.
- It has a postscript (PS) at the end.

All of these are features of letters rather than other types of texts.

**2** In what ways does it not look like a letter? (2 marks)

Advice

You might mention:

- the image of a rehydration sachet at the top of the letter
- the use of underlined headings
- the image of the child at the foot of the letter

Play safe: given that two marks are available, aim to make two points, preferably both within one sentence.

**3** Say in one sentence what you think the main purpose of the letter is. (2 marks)

B

The main aim is to encourage readers to make a donation to the charity.

**4** This is a long letter, and it is important that the writer manages to hold our attention. How successfully does the writer use layout to keep us interested? (6 marks)

The text uses various devices to look more visually interesting. On the opening page it has an image of a rehydration sachet with a caption in small print beside it. This gives the letter a factual feel, and also makes us curious to know more. The main heading is in lower case letters, but is in bold print and underlined: it dominates the page and makes us want to read on.

The writer then uses brief paragraphs to keep our eye moving down the page. Sometimes, for emphasis, these paragraphs are just one sentence long – often to create a dramatic impact: 'But despite these hardships, Celestine faced an even greater challenge'.

The frequent use of short paragraphs could become quite repetitive, but the writer tries to make them more visually interesting with further layout features – bold, underlined subheadings ('But these children are dying needlessly,' for example) and bold text at the beginning of paragraphs ('But still children are dying', for example). This adds variety to the appearance of the letter.

All of these techniques of layout help to hold our interest and make the letter more visually interesting. Overall the use of layout is quite successful, but I think the letter is probably too long and the second page in particular needs more interesting use of layout to hold our attention.

Advice

This answer describes the layout features well. It uses specific terms like 'bold' and 'subheadings', and supports these with examples. The answer addresses both parts of the question too, including how successful the use of layout is. A less skilful answer would spot features but not then evaluate how successfully they are used. There might still be more detail here about what the writer could do to make the layout more successful – or perhaps how the writer might cut the letter to make it more effective.

**5** The writer hopes that we will become emotionally involved in the dreadful conditions he describes and will become regular supporters of Save the Children's work. What techniques are used to persuade us to help, and how successful overall do you find the letter? (8 marks)

The writer of the letter aims to get us emotionally involved by addressing us as 'Dear Friend'. This suggests that we are already supporters of the charity – or at least people who would probably want to be supporters. The writer writes to 'you', once again giving the impression that we are personally involved.

To get our involvement in the stories of Erisa and Celestine, the writer shows how terrible their life is. He uses quite dramatic words to help us to imagine this: 'massacre', 'wracked', 'painful death'. These details are shocking to read and come as a surprise after the factual tone at the start, which described what a rehydration sachet could do.

The writer is skilful in showing the connection between the suffering of the girls and the dehydration sachet. It gives a feeling of hope – that there is something that can be done. Having shown us this, the writer makes a direct appeal for our financial help, underlining the request for added emphasis.

Overall these techniques are successful in persuading us to help. The only thing which, in my opinion, doesn't work, is the length of the letter. I think it is too long and would not definitely hold the reader's attention from beginning to end.

Advice

This is a tricky question, which needs a lot of attention to the language of the text. Notice also that it has two parts – how the writer persuades us, and how successful you think the letter is. The sample answer addresses both parts of the question, but could probably go into more detail about how the letter might be shorter. Even so, it is a well-constructed answer.

# Section 2

# Broader comparisons: questions and sample answers

# Broader Questions

pages 10–18

## Leaflets

Your work will be assessed on the quality of your Reading.

The RSPCA and Greenpeace leaflets both attempt to persuade their readers to support their campaign.

Explain and analyse the techniques used in the leaflets to achieve this.

(Reading 16 marks)

Advice

Look at the images used in each leaflet. How are animals portrayed in each? What about the humans? What message are these images giving?

Look at the layout of each leaflet: how the text is divided up, the length of paragraphs, the use of headings and subheadings. What words, phrases, slogans or images stand out most?

Look at the language used in the text. What words are used to describe the work of each organization? Do the leaflets rely on recounting stories or listing facts, to get their arguments across? What effect do their styles have?

Look at the vocabulary – is it straightforward or complex? What can you tell about who the leaflets are aimed at? Do they use emotional words to persuade us to support the cause?

pages 19–26

## Leaflets comparison

Your work will be assessed on the quality of your Reading.

The leaflets produced by supermarkets Waitrose and Tesco both encourage us to eat more healthily. Analyse the similarities and differences in the techniques they use. (Reading 16 marks)

Advice

Remember that the leaflets have different audiences and purposes. The Tesco leaflet is intended to encourage parents to provide children with a healthy diet. The Waitrose leaflet aims to make adults think more about their own diets. Look for ways in which the different purpose and audience come through – in the design, the images and styles of artwork, and the language.

There are two basic approaches to answering this question:

You could:

- spend the first half of your answer writing about text A (the Tesco leaflet), and the second half talking about text B (the Waitrose leaflet);
- write about the layout in text A; then the layout in text B; then the language in text A; then the language in text B; then conclude with a summary of the similarities and the differences between them.

pages 27–36

## Reportage

Your work will be assessed on the quality of your Reading.

The newspaper article from the Daily Express and George Orwell's essay both describe ways that humans treat animals.

Explain and analyse how the writers present the human beings and their attitudes to the animals in the passages. (Reading 16 marks)

Advice

Start by making lists – the way the humans are presented in each text and their attitude to animals.

Look at the attitude of the writer to the people in the texts – is it poking fun, sneering, admiring, racist?

How much description of the animals is there in each passage?

Focus on the language of the texts – words used to describe the people and their attitudes to the animals.

pages 38–43

## Reportage comparison 2

Your work will be assessed on the quality of your Reading.

These two newspaper reports come from different newspapers – one a broadsheet (sometimes called a 'quality' newspaper); the other a tabloid. Write about the similarities and differences you notice in the way the story is presented in the two reports. (Reading 16 marks)

Advice

Plan carefully by making lists of what you notice in each report. Write them down under two headings – similarities and differences. This will help you to organize a clear answer.

Make sure you discuss the language used in each text as well as the content.

Look in particular at the way each report tells the story. Which grabs your attention more and why?

pages 44–51

## Autobiography

Your work will be assessed on the quality of your Reading.

The extracts from 'My Mam's Death' and 'Cursed' both recall strongly emotional memories from the writers' lives.

Explain and analyse what we learn about the characters of the two writers from the extracts. (Reading 16 marks)

Advice

**Text A**

Look at the way the writer tells her story – in quite a matter-of-fact way, especially at the beginning.

What does she show us of her relationship with her mother and other members of her family? How does this help her to tell her story?

Look at the vocabulary she uses – 'loads of' and 'no way'. What effect does this informal style have on what we learn about her?

**Text B**

Look at the way the writer describes being treated by his family – for example his grandmother and parents. What effect might this have had? How does he describe his feelings?

Look at the thoughts he has about the Nottingham Goose Fair – what does this show about his self-confidence? How does he describe these memories?

Look at the thoughts he has about God.

Is the whole passage written in the same style, or does it vary?

pages 52–63

## Travel writing

Your work will be assessed on the quality of your Reading.

In 'Hitching Through the Yukon' and 'A Desert Dies' we are shown two very contrasting environments. Explain and analyse how the writers create a strong sense of place. (Reading 16 marks)

Advice

**Text A**

Look at the opening paragraph, which gives the reader background information about the place.

Comment on how she describes people and places throughout the passage – is it with a lot of detail or a lightly-sketched approach?

**Text B**

Look at the descriptions of the desert and the storm.

Notice how visual this author's language is – and how aggressive the storm is. This helps us to feel that we are there with him.

Look at the way he uses Arab words to help create the flavour of the place.

pages 64–70

## Campaigning advertisements

Your work will be assessed on the quality of your Reading.

The advertisements for the Samaritans and Sight Savers International use different techniques to achieve different ends, through newspaper advertisements.

Explain and analyse the techniques they use. (Reading 16 marks)

Advice

Plan your answer before you start writing: make a list of layout points and a list of language points.

Are any images used? What are they like, and what message do they give?

Talk about who the advertisements seem to be aimed at – how can you tell?

Discuss their tone – calm, reassuring, serious... How are they supposed to make us feel?

Comment on the length of paragraphs, the types of sentences, the vocabulary: how do they all help persuade us?

pages 71–81

## Biography

Your work will be assessed on the quality of your Reading.

The passages about Sally Gunnell and the Detective both aim to make the lives of two people vivid.

Analyse and explore the techniques used in the two passages to present their subjects. (Reading 16 marks)

Advice

**Text A**

Look at the way the writer begins. She doesn't start at the beginning of Sally Gunnell's life. Instead she begins with a key moment from her adult career. Why is this and what effect does it have?

How does the writer describe people and places to help us imagine that we are there?

Look at how she gives us information about Sally Gunnell's thoughts and feelings, as well as telling us about her public life. How does this help us to feel that we know Sally Gunnell?

Notice that she calls her subject 'Sally' rather than 'Sally Gunnell'. Why do you think this is?

**Text B**

You need to be able to say what George Barrett is like. Look at how the writer tells his story – showing Barrett in different situations, in places which are vividly described.

The text feels different from normal biographies. Try to keep showing how the writer is working in an unusual way – for example, not giving us very much information about Barrett; instead letting us learn about him by watching him do his job.

pages 82–93

## Information texts

Your work will be assessed on the quality of your Reading.

These two texts are intended to inform readers about health and fitness, and about aircraft technology.

Analyse and explore the techniques they use to get information across.

(Reading 16 marks)

Advice

Select the important information you'll need from the text.

Use brief quotations from the text to support your ideas.

Look at the layout of the texts – how the writers organize the information.

Look at the way that language is used. How are sentences constructed to keep the information clear? How difficult or technical is the vocabulary?

Look for ways in which the writer adds any hints of human interest – stories of events involving people – to keep the reader's attention.

Look also at the use of charts in the texts. How clear is the information presented in this way? How does it help the reader?

pages 94–101

## Advertorials

Your work will be assessed on the quality of your Reading.

The texts use the format of newspaper articles to advertise their products.

Compare and analyse the techniques they use to persuade us to buy them.

(Reading 16 marks)

Advice

**Text A**

Comment on the way it looks like a newspaper – the photograph, caption, headline, columns, and so on.

Look at the headline and caption in more detail – do they sound like newspaper style?

As you read the main text, look for clues that the writer is trying to create the effect of a newspaper. Can you spot sections where it is obviously an advertisement?

**Text B**

Look at the layout of the advertisement – why do you think it uses the format of a newspaper story? What impression does this give of the product?

Look at the headline and caption in more detail – do they sound like newspaper style?

Comment on who you think the advertisement is aimed at. How can you tell?

What do we learn about the product? How does the advertisement make it seem relevant to us?

Remember all the time to comment closely on the language of the extract – the words, tone and sentences.

pages 102–108

## Comparison by theme

Your work will be assessed on the quality of your Reading.

These two texts are both on the theme of computers. Explore the similarities and differences you notice between the two texts.

(Reading 16 marks)

Advice

Careful planning is vital – decide how you are going to organize your response. You might have a paragraph about what we learn about computers in each text; another about the purpose of each text; another about the written styles of the texts... and so on.

Aim for a five- to six-point paragraph plan.

Your conclusion should summarize the similarities and differences you notice.

pages 109–118

## Letters

Your work will be assessed on the quality of your Reading.

These two letters are written for very different purposes. Analyse and explore the similarities and differences you notice between them – in who they are written for, what their purpose is, and the language they use.

(Reading 16 marks)

Advice

Start by making a list of headings for each point: audience, purpose, style. Look for similarities and differences.

How can you tell that text A is more personal? How would you describe its purpose?

What techniques does text B use to persuade its readers to support its campaign? Look at the use of layout as well as language.

Structure your answer so that you keep comparing the two letters for each point (audience, purpose, style) rather than writing the first half of your answer about text A and the second half about text B.

# Broader Answers

pages 10–18

## Leaflets

Your work will be assessed on the quality of your Reading.

The RSPCA and Greenpeace leaflets both attempt to persuade their readers to support their campaign.

Explain and analyse the techniques used in the leaflets to achieve this.

(Reading 16 marks)

Your answer might include these points:

| *Text A: RSPCA leaflet* | *Text B: Greenpeace leaflet* |
|---|---|
| Sad-looking dog to gain our attention. | Image – human helping netted seal – shows Greenpeace does things. |
| Smiling RSPCA officer to show caring, friendly attitude. | Headlines stress actions – shows an active organization. |
| Emphasis on telling stories – e.g. Trio's story – to get us emotionally involved in a specific example of abuse. | Short paragraphs to keep us reading. |
| Emotional words like 'smashing', 'petrified', 'cruel'. | 'Action' emphasized in bold to reinforce the message. |
| Letter to persuade us to help – includes statistics about the work of the RSPCA. | Images of action – speedboat, etc. |
| List of the kind of work the RSPCA does – makes us more likely to support it. | List of the different campaigns Greenpeace runs – shows the breadth of their work. |
| Image of crossed-out pound sign and sentence, 'We receive no government funding', emphasizes how important donations are. | Powerful visual language – 'scaling chimneys that pump out toxic emissions...' – emphasizes the danger of their work and how badly needed it is. |
| | 'History of the planet' section – shows the wonder of life on Earth, and how humans are ruining it. |

A good answer will be clearly organized, probably with a different paragraph based on each new topic – for example, one paragraph on use of images, one on layout, one on language.

You could spend half your answer writing about one leaflet and half about the other. However, a better answer will try to compare the two leaflets more directly – a paragraph about the use of images in the RSPCA leaflet, followed by a paragraph about the images in the Greenpeace leaflet; then a paragraph about the layout of the RSPCA leaflet followed by the same theme in the Greenpeace leaflet... and so on. This will produce a more systematic comparison.

You need to keep using phrases like 'The writer persuades us to feel sympathy by...' and 'This is another way that we are persuaded to feel sympathy...'. Phrases like these convince the examiner that you are tackling the question directly.

**Sample: opening paragraph**

Look at this example of a good opening paragraph, which focuses on the images used in the RSPCA leaflet:

states area paragraph will deal with

moves on to content

The RSPCA leaflet uses images which immediately catch our attention and make us feel sympathy for the animals. It shows three images of different dogs, all of which feature in the text of the leaflet. In one picture we can clearly see the dog has had to have a leg amputated. In another, the dog looks very weak and thin. The pictures are not too disturbing but they suggest these animals have suffered. In contrast, the photo at the centre of the leaflet shows a happier looking dog with a smiling RSPCA officer. This suggests to us that the RSPCA can make suffering animals happier. Even before we begin to read the text, we begin to get this message.

shows effect of content

# Broader Answers

pages 19–26

## Leaflets comparison

Your work will be assessed on the quality of your Reading.

The leaflets produced by supermarkets Waitrose and Tesco both encourage us to eat more healthily. Analyse the similarities and differences in the techniques they use. (Reading 16 marks)

Your answer might include these points:

| *Text A: Tesco leaflet* | *Text B: Waitrose leaflet* |
|---|---|
| Clear organization of different topics – fats, sugars and teeth, etc. | Clear organization by different types of food – fruit and vegetables, meat and fish, etc. |
| Use of cartoons to add visual interest. | More adult, less childish style of artwork than Tesco leaflet. |
| Clear explanation at the start of why healthy eating for children is important. | Colour adds visual interest. |
| Clear instruction using commands: 'Make sure... keep sweets... dilute fruit juices...'. This creates a direct tone. | More technical information on what people should eat and why. |
| Useful list of ten tips to make it all sound quite straightforward. | Guidance on how to read nutrition information on food labels. Instructions phrased as suggestions rather than commands: 'Try to...', 'Opt for...'. |

**Sample: comparing two texts in detail**

Notice how the following extract from an answer is organized. The writer has structured it into a series of paragraphs. Each paragraph concentrates on one aspect of both leaflets: their aim, content, and artwork. A good answer would also include detail on the language of the leaflets.

[paragraph focusing on aim]

The Tesco leaflet (text A) is about children but it is not aimed at children. It is aimed at parents. It says, for example, 'Give your children fruit...'. It is intended to educate parents. The Waitrose leaflet (text B) is also aimed at adults, but as well as aiming to educate parents it tries to build up a partnership between writer and reader: 'Should we avoid certain foods altogether?'

[writer looks at similarity] [writer then looks at key differences] [on content]

The advice in both leaflets is similar – for example, the need to cut down sugar and fat. However, the Tesco leaflet places more stress on the needs of young children and summarizes its advice on the 'tips' section at the back. The Waitrose leaflet gives more technical information. It talks about 'kilojoules' and 'kilocalories' and shows how to read nutrition labels. This is another sign that it is aimed completely at adults.

[good example of technical language]

on artwork

The Tesco leaflet has a brighter, more eye-catching design, perhaps because it is talking about children's habits. The illustrations have the feel of cartoons, and the 'tips' headline is made up from children's magnetic letters. This makes it all feel informal and quite light-hearted. The design of the Waitrose leaflet is more serious. It does use attractive images of fruit, vegetables and fish, and its main pages are dominated by the plate of different healthy foodstuffs. However although the design makes it clear and quite informal, it is not at all light-hearted, especially when compared to the Tesco leaflet.

good, clear comparison

# Broader Answers

pages 27–36

## Reportage

Your work will be assessed on the quality of your Reading.

The newspaper article from the Daily Express and George Orwell's essay both describe ways that humans treat animals.

Explain and analyse how the writers present the human beings and their attitudes to the animals in the passages. (Reading 16 marks)

Your answer might include the following points:

| *Text A: Daily Express newspaper report* | *Text B: George Orwell eyewitness account* |
|---|---|
| Description of the way the huntsmen are dressed – 'spruced up' – shows their wealth. | Description of narrator – anxious, uncertain of whether to follow his instincts ('I did not want to shoot the elephant') or the wishes of the onlookers. |
| Pokes fun at the hunters a bit – for example the image of their wedding cake. | Mistrust of crowd. |
| Pokes fun also at the way they speak. | Racist attitude to 'natives'. |
| Huntsman seems to admire foxes – 'they really are clever'. | Admiration for elephant. |
| Doesn't show hunters as cruel – 'we don't actually catch that many'. | Sickening feeling about what he has done to the creature – sympathy for the elephant. |
| The monitors are described in quite a neutral way – shows their commitment to the cause and desire to protect animals – 'We'll never get a perfect world while humans are in it'. | Disgust at behaviour of Burmese, stripping the body. |

**Sample: using quotations to support your points**

The best answers will give specific examples to support their ideas. For example, you might be commenting on the way the writer of text A, Lynne Wallis, describes the hunters – this is a clue to how she feels about hunting. Here's how to support points with quotations:

first sentence summarizes whole paragraph

quote from text

effect of quote – what it tells us

I think the writer pokes fun at the hunters a bit. When she describes Marilyn Husbands saying, 'I'm terribly ordinary', she adds in brackets: 'three times'. This suggests someone who is a bit of a bore. She also quotes one of the hunters saying, 'Oh no, she's fallen orf'. This seems to be mocking the upper class language they use. Her last paragraph says, 'I didn't hear one single "Tally ho!" all day'. Again, I think this is poking fun at the hunters – showing what she expected them to be like – even though she seems to be making no judgement about 'right, wrong, nice or nasty'.

### Sample: writing about a writer's attitude

In the next example, the student has picked out particular quotations to support a point – here, about George Orwell's attitude to the Burmese people who watch him shooting the elephant:

focus on effect of specific words

The description of the people seems quite racist. Orwell describes the 'yellow faces' of the crowd, and emphasizes how isolated he feels by saying, 'A white man mustn't be frightened in front of "natives".' He describes the Burmese people through labels – 'natives' – rather than making them seem individual or human. When the gun goes off he describes the 'devilish roar of glee' from the crowd. The word 'devilish' shows his clear dislike of the people and, in particular, the way they are enjoying this spectacle. At the end he describes the way the people scavenge over the body – 'they had stripped his body almost to the bones by the afternoon'. His emotions here are contempt for their attitude and behaviour, disbelief that they can behave like this, and a feeling of loathing shown in his choice of words.

what quotation shows us

quotation

### Sample: comparing texts

Knowing how to compare texts can be difficult. Your answer can feel very disjointed – hopping from one text to the next to make a point. Look at this sample and notice how it handles the material:

opening statement

both texts compared in one sentence

The two texts have few similarities, in content or style. Lynne Wallis's article presents a picture of a group of people, whereas George Orwell deals with his own story and the emotions he feels. His text is therefore more direct because we trace what he sees and thinks. His text is also more emotional. Lynne Wallis stays quite neutral about what she thinks of hunting. She says, 'right, wrong, nice or nasty' at the end of her article, but doesn't say which of the words best describes her feelings. She pokes fun at the language of the hunters a bit – 'she's fallen orf' – which could suggest that she's on the side of the hunt monitors. But she avoids revealing her feelings directly.

more detail on Orwell

more detail on Wallis

back to Orwell

George Orwell's emotions, on the other hand, are much more in evidence. In the first half of his description he says, 'I was not afraid in the ordinary sense'. This is because he knows he is being watched, so he tries to hide his fear. Later in the extract he uses emotive words like 'frightful' and 'painfully' to show us that the elephant is suffering. George Orwell obviously sympathizes with the elephant's pain strongly because he says, 'I felt that I had got to put an end to that dreadful noise.'

Notice how useful phrases like 'on the other hand' can be in answers like this. They can signal to the reader that you are changing the direction of your argument, or moving on to a different text.

# Broader Answers

pages 38–43

## Reportage comparison 2

Your work will be assessed on the quality of your Reading.

These two newspaper reports come from different newspapers – one a broadsheet (sometimes called a 'quality' newspaper); the other a tabloid. Write about the similarities and differences you notice in the way the story is presented in the two reports. (Reading 16 marks)

Your answer might include the following points:

| *Text A: tabloid* | *Text B: broadsheet* |
|---|---|
| Shorter and more dramatic wording in headline – 'dash', 'saves'. | More detail of actual story in headline: 'Pilot flies below bridges'. |
| Use of strapline to give more information on what actually happened: 'We skimmed waves...'. | No strapline. |
| Opening paragraph has phrase 'wave hopped' – sounds highly dangerous and daring. | Opening paragraph gives more detail of story – flying beneath power cables. |
| No illustration. | Illustration to show what happened. |
| Simpler vocabulary: 'divers... suffering from the bends' in first paragraph. | More technical: 'potentially lethal pressure changes' in first paragraph. |
| Overall, quite simple vocabulary and shorter words. | Overall, longer and more complex words: 'precipitate or exacerbate the condition', 'precautionary measure', 'hyperbaric'. Suggests more educated readership. |
| Twins' attempt to rescue third diver just mentioned in passing. | More stress on what happened to the third diver whom they were trying to rescue. |
| Only one quote from eyewitness. | More eyewitness statements included – two crew plus doctor – gives sense of being more thoroughly researched. |
| References to other incidents at quarry. | No mention of other, similar accidents. |
| Shorter report. | Longer and more detailed report. |

# Broader Answers

pages 44–51

## Autobiography

Your work will be assessed on the quality of your Reading.

The extracts from 'My Mam's Death' and 'Cursed' both recall strongly emotional memories from the writers' lives.

Explain and analyse what we learn about the characters of the two writers from the extracts. (Reading 16 marks)

Your answer might include the following points:

| *Text A: My Mam's Death* | *Text B: Cursed* |
|---|---|
| Early part – concerned about her mother but quite optimistic (hopeful). | Hurt and confused by comments of grandmother. |
| Works hard to make house welcoming for her mother – compassion. | Suffers lack of affection from parents. |
| Deeply affected by her mother's death – 'my life just fell apart'. | Hates pressure to be tough. |
| Strong – puts her life back together. | Very low self-esteem – compares himself to 'freaks' / thinks he might be drowned. |
| | Feels his life might not last long. |

**Sample: focusing on language**

A strong answer will also look at the language the writers use, showing how this reveals their characters – for example:

tone

Text A is very moving and emotional, and yet Samantha Studley writes in quite a controlled way. The opening sentence sets the factual tone, and leads into a step-by-step account of what happened. But when the focus shifts to the narrator at home preparing for her mother's return, the text becomes more emotional, showing how upset the girl is: Samantha Studley talks about 'shattering news' and 'sheer hell', and this choice of vocabulary is a contrast to the earlier more factual account. The description of the period after the mother's death returns to a fairly factual style, chiefly just cataloguing what happened. Overall the vocabulary has an informal feeling – words like 'moped' and 'should've' – which helps us to visualize the teenage girl who has suffered. Towards the end her style feels a bit more formal – 'gradually I picked up the shattered pieces of my torn life'.

examples of emotional language

vocabulary

style

structure of sentences

David Swift also writes in a style which is quite informal, but with a difference: the text actually sounds more like spoken language at times – for example, 'I felt as if, well, as if...'. The style here is almost chatty. It isn't clear who he is addressing, but it feels as if he may be speaking aloud, perhaps to himself, as a way of coming to terms with his experiences. Quite a few sentences begin with the conjunctions 'and', 'but' and 'so', and this gives the text an informal feel. This makes me think that David Swift may actually be thinking aloud, rather than writing a formal autobiography. On the other hand, sometimes David Swift uses

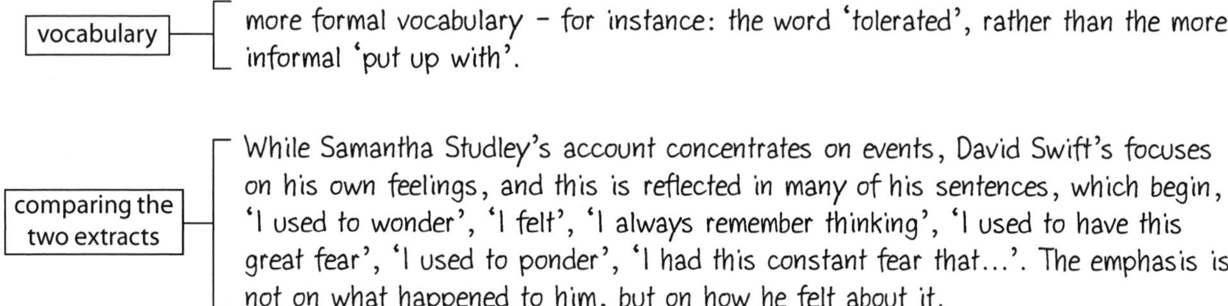

vocabulary — more formal vocabulary – for instance: the word 'tolerated', rather than the more informal 'put up with'.

comparing the two extracts — While Samantha Studley's account concentrates on events, David Swift's focuses on his own feelings, and this is reflected in many of his sentences, which begin, 'I used to wonder', 'I felt', 'I always remember thinking', 'I used to have this great fear', 'I used to ponder', 'I had this constant fear that...'. The emphasis is not on what happened to him, but on how he felt about it.

# Broader Answers

pages 52–63

## Travel writing

Your work will be assessed on the quality of your Reading.
In 'Hitching Through the Yukon' and 'A Desert Dies' we are shown two very contrasting environments. Explain and analyse how the writers create a strong sense of place. (Reading 16 marks)

Your answer might include the following points:

| *Text A: Hitching through the Yukon* | *Text B: A Desert Dies* |
|---|---|
| Details – population and type of landscape. | Highly descriptive vocabulary – 'savage sand-storm punched into us...' |
| Emphasizes distances – showing size of the territory. | Arab words help us to feel the drama and excitement of the landscape. |
| Shows the Yukon has a powerful effect on people – people who came to visit remain to live there. | Emphasizes the power of nature. |
| Description of dust suggests heat. | Shows danger of the landscape – hazard of getting lost. |
| Writer's style uses a light rather than detailed descriptive approach. | Describes how well the Arab travellers understand the landscape – and how alien it feels to him. |

**Sample: commenting upon images**

Michael Asher's writing is highly visual, and a good answer should confidently explore the way he creates pictures in his language. Look at some of his images and what you might say about them.

'a savage sand-storm punched into us with hammer force'

'Punched' creates the impression that the storm is human and that it is attacking people on purpose.

'Hammer force' suggests the storm has all the solid force of a blow from a physical object.

'sand that streaked across the surface like currents of electricity'

This suggests that the sand moves rapidly across the dunes, making a wave formation like that of an electric current. Associating the sand with electricity reinforces the impression of its power and speed.

'disappearing into the veil of dust'

'Veil of dust' suggests a thin shroud. Although the dust is fine, it has the power to make humans disappear.

'The golden beams of the dwindling sun spread out... like the arms of a giant starfish'

There is a conflict here between 'dwindling' (shrinking) and 'spread out': the force of the sun is fading with evening but at the same time its rays seem to reach across the sky.

'Like the arms of a giant starfish' - an unusual image in a piece of writing about a desert - conjuring up ideas of the sea.

Overall, a serene image, contrasting with the earlier, violent images of the storm.

# Broader Answers

pages 64–70

## Campaigning advertisements

Your work will be assessed on the quality of your Reading.

The advertisements for the Samaritans and Sight Savers International use different techniques to achieve different ends, through newspaper advertisements.

Explain and analyse the techniques they use. (Reading 16 marks)

Your answer might include the following points:

| *Text A: The Samaritans* | *Text B: Sight Savers International* |
|---|---|
| Large image to catch our eye. | Very eye-catching image – barbed wire eyelashes. |
| Slogan designed to make us pause because it challenges our expectations – normally we would expect to talk to someone we like rather than don't like. | Striking headline. |
| Short paragraphs to hold our interest. | Short paragraphs to hold our interest. |
| Chatty style – gets us involved and makes us feel we can trust the Samaritans. | Dramatic language to describe unpleasant experiences – builds our sympathy. |
| Speaks directly to reader but doesn't use true stories of people who've needed help. Instead suggests that it's okay to talk about problems. | Tells stories of particular individuals to attract interest. |
| Aims to encourage people with problems to seek help. | Aims to raise money. |
| Aimed particularly at young men. | Aimed at adult readers of either sex. |
| Addressed to 'you' all the time – makes it feel directly aimed at us. | Personal pronoun 'you' to make us feel involved. |

**Sample: writing about layout**

It's important that your answer spends time discussing both the layout and the language. Sometimes students spend too long on layout because they find it more straightforward.

When writing about layout you need to be as precise as possible, describing what you notice:

The layout of the Samaritans advertisement centres on a large image of a young woman who appears to be smiling. The question inside the photograph box suggests that this is an image of a girlfriend. This tells us something about the target audience of the advertisement – it seems to be aimed at young men.

This is good because it says what the student has noticed – and then relates this to the audience or purpose of the advertisement. Remember to keep talking about the 'advertisement' – not the 'advert'.

**Sample: looking at how language is used to persuade**

You will often be asked to write about language which has been used to persuade or influence the reader. Here is a sample:

first sentence

The first sentence of the Sight Savers advertisement leaves us feeling unsure of what is happening. It is as if we are joining the middle of a conversation and it is not clear what the pronoun 'it' is referring to. This is a good way of drawing us quickly into the text: it makes us keen to read on to find out what is not too bad.

next section

The text then goes on to describe the process of the disease. It takes us, step by step, through the way trachoma develops. The language is fairly informal – 'it's' and 'don't' instead of the more formal version of these words – and this helps to hold our interest. The language creates a feeling of how simple the process is: 'And that's all it takes to spread trachoma'. I think that this makes us realize how difficult it must be to avoid the disease. It makes us see the people who get it as helpless victims.

change from 'they' to 'you'

The really big shift in language is from 'they' to 'you' – as in 'You only notice there's something wrong...' Suddenly the text has changed. Instead of our being outside looking in on the disease, we are part of the scene, looking at a child suffering. This is a very powerful device which makes us feel very involved in the text.

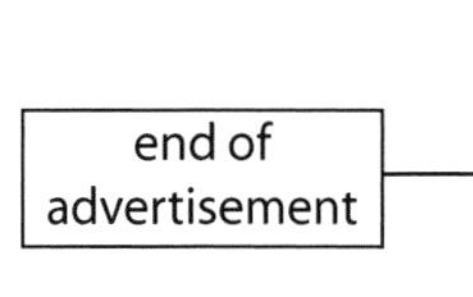


The later part of the advertisement goes on to show us how easy the suffering would be to avoid – this is the 'utterly horrifying thing' about it. It then goes on to show how cheap a cure can be. The final section uses figures to persuade us how easy it would be for us to help, and explains how different sums of money could have a different effect. To encourage us to make a contribution the advertisement uses a question: 'Wouldn't you pay a hundred or a thousand times that if it were your eyes at stake?' Having shown us how little we need to contribute, the writer then makes us think about our own values and hints that if we don't pay we would be being selfish. It is an effective method for persuading us.

This answer keeps closely to the text. It is very observant and supports each point with quotations. Notice how each paragraph ends with a statement about the effect of the language features the reader has analysed.

# Broader Answers

pages 71–81

## Biography

Your work will be assessed on the quality of your Reading.

The passages about Sally Gunnell and the Detective both aim to make the lives of two people vivid.

Analyse and explore the techniques used in the two passages to present their subjects. (Reading 16 marks)

Your answer might include the following points:

| *Text A: Sally Gunnell* | *Text B: The Detective* |
|---|---|
| Starts with a specific event – the Barcelona Olympics – to draw us in. | Follows George Barrett's routines as a way of showing what kind of person he is. |
| Creates an initial sense of drama. | Shows him in different contexts to illuminate different parts of his character – e.g. at home with his family, then on the streets. |
| Not much background detail beyond first sentence: 'It was a hot August day...' | Vivid descriptions of place, and of the criminals he is after, help us visualize the conditions he works in – e.g. the 'sewer' of Broadway. |
| Shows us the talent and determination of Sally Gunnell, then more about her as a person – for example, what she eats. | Fragmented narrative allows the writer to cut between scenes – including a flashback to childhood – giving us a fuller picture. |
| Uses simple clear language to make it easy to follow. | Writer doesn't try to be flattering – tells it straight. |
| Shows us Sally Gunnell's thoughts and feelings to help us feel that we know her. | Refers to him as 'Barrett' or 'George Barrett' – never 'George' alone – so quite distant impression of him. |
| Refers to her as 'Sally' to make her sound familiar to readers. | Uses language and description to give physical impression of George Barrett: eyes 'cold as gun metal', jaw 'hard and square as a brick', etc. |
| Uses photographs to give physical impression of Sally Gunnell – running, winning medal. No description of her. | Overall tone: dark, sinister, detailed – but also exciting? |
| Overall tone: bright, up-beat. | |

As always, try to make your answer as specific as possible. Best answers usually contain a quotation every two or three lines to support each point.

**Sample: analysing a writer's language**

The best answers will look not just at the subject of the passage, but at the writer's use of language in portraying him:

quote

The writer of text B uses descriptive visual language – 'the flashing neon fireball of Times Square'. His language makes the place seem fascinating and yet unpleasant, partly because of the dramatic, negative words used – such as 'sewer' and 'germs'. This shows us how Barrett views the scene and it has the feeling of a jungle. The writer uses words like 'prowling' and 'hunting' to make it all feel wild and dangerous.

focus on specific words

The writer lists other details, moving through them quickly. He doesn't describe any of the criminals in detail – he just creates an impression – the prostitutes, pimps and car boosters. He describes the last group in more detail, but always shows them as a group. We never get a picture of the individuals involved in the crime. For this reason, the criminals feel impersonal and, again, animal-like, carefully calculating their next move and attack.

As a result, we can sense how exciting the scene is, as well as how dangerous.

He describes the different types of people on the street, including prostitutes who sit with 'velvet chairs and phony flowers'. This detail hints at the fact that they try to look high class – 'velvet' – but are actually quite cheap – 'phony flowers'.

quote

The writer uses quite a lot of lists to show the variety of the scene. It has a lively, bustling feel because of phrases like this: 'vicious cousins, the A&R men, assault and robbery specialists, muggers'. The streets are teeming with life, and the lists emphasize this impression.

quote

# Broader Answers

pages 82–93

## Information texts

Your work will be assessed on the quality of your Reading.

These two texts are intended to inform readers about health and fitness, and about aircraft technology.

Analyse and explore the techniques they use to get information across.

(Reading 16 marks)

Your answer might include the following points:

| *Text A: Health and Fitness: Enjoying Exercise* | *Text B: Aircraft Technology: Airliners* |
|---|---|
| General introduction includes a table so that people can find out about specific sports they are interested in. | History of aircraft is clearly told so that each paragraph deals with a different part of their development. |
| Table uses easy-to-follow scale. | Quite a few technical terms (e.g. 'monoplanes') suggest that it may be for someone who already knows something about the subject. |
| Friendly style – reader is addressed as 'you', to make him/her feel involved. | Feature explains how supersonic flight works – describes a scientific process in fairly straightforward terms. |
| Clear written style shows the readers the benefits and disadvantages of different sports, giving them information so that they can make up their own minds. | Strong factual content – lots of statistics. Little information on the people behind the development of aircraft – few stories/anecdotes. Impersonal style. |
| Some more complex vocabulary, e.g. 'conceivable', 'competitive' – may be aimed at adult reader. | |

**Sample: writing critically about texts**

It is important to write not just about what is in a text but also what you think of it – including what its weaknesses are and how it might be improved. In the case of information texts, if you feel information is unclear or details aren't explained, you will gain marks by saying so. For example:

focus on content

style

vocabulary

Text B contains a lot more technical information. It gives plenty of specific points about dates and types of aeroplane, and about advances in aircraft development. The style the writer uses is quite a direct one, though also impersonal. The sentences feel well-controlled and informative – as in the first paragraph. The vocabulary is mostly straightforward, though the writer could explain technical terms like 'monoplanes' (he does explain biplanes, earlier, by saying 'two-winged aeroplanes…').

reader has identified unexplained term

# Broader Answers

pages 94–101

## Advertorials

Your work will be assessed on the quality of your Reading.

The texts use the format of newspaper articles to advertise their products.

Compare and analyse the techniques they use to persuade us to buy them. (Reading 16 marks)

Your answer might include the following points:

| *Text A: Norwich Union advertorial* | *Text B: Memory advertorial* |
|---|---|
| Uses layout features of newspaper articles to make us want to read Louise's story – photograph, headline, sub-headings, short paragraphs. | Uses layout features of newspaper articles to capture our attention – photograph, headline, sub-headings, |
| Bullet-points of advice in 'Guy Fawkes' column make it seem less obviously an advertising piece. | Language style is not like newspaper article – more similar to 'straight' advertising. |
| Uses word-play in main headline to imitate newspaper style and make us want to read on. | Emphasizes the disadvantages of a poor memory to show how the advanced memory technique could help readers. |
| Language style in first half of advertisement is very similar to newspaper style. | Lists the many benefits – such as never forgetting appointments, learning names – and emphasizes a wide range of possibilities to attract as many people as possible. Advert is not built around single story. |
| Uses a specific example – Louise White – to show the benefits of insurance. Advert is built around story. | Encourages readers to send for a free booklet as a next step – they don't have to buy anything yet. |
| Phone number ('call free') repeated three times, for emphasis. | |

The key to doing well with this question is knowing about the style of newspapers. If you don't feel confident about this, look at the newspaper summary sheet on pages 89 and 90.

### Sample: analysing newspaper style

Notice how in this sample the student constantly compares each feature of the advertisements with newspaper styles and approaches. This sort of systematic answer will gain marks in an exam.

format | strapline | headline | pun

The advertisement probably uses the format of a newspaper article to draw newspaper readers in – perhaps before they realize that they are reading an advertisement. The headline in Text A is similar to a real newspaper article's. It uses a fairly corny pun – 'Aisle' instead of 'I'll' – which is something that tabloid newspapers quite often do. The strapline – 'Boost for Bride Lou' – also

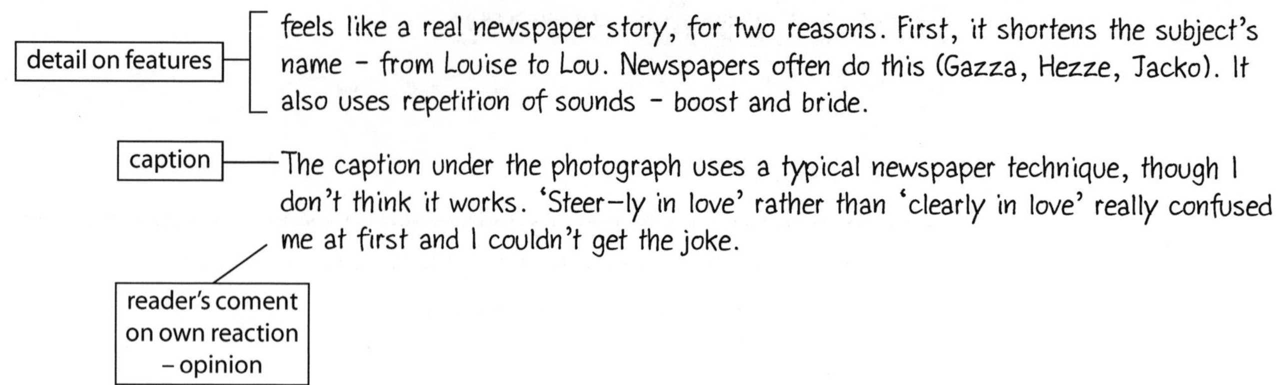


feels like a real newspaper story, for two reasons. First, it shortens the subject's name – from Louise to Lou. Newspapers often do this (Gazza, Hezze, Jacko). It also uses repetition of sounds – boost and bride.

The caption under the photograph uses a typical newspaper technique, though I don't think it works. 'Steer–ly in love' rather than 'clearly in love' really confused me at first and I couldn't get the joke.

# Broader Answers

pages 102–108

## Comparison by theme

Your work will be assessed on the quality of your Reading.

These two texts are both on the theme of computers. Explore the similarities and differences you notice between the two texts.

(Reading 16 marks)

| *Text A: Adam Woodyatt article* | *Text B: Comet information booklet* |
|---|---|
| Text written by one person about his experiences with computers – very personal, informal, autobiographical style. Use of word 'I'. Photo of author included to reinforce sense of who he is. | Style is informal but impersonal – no sense of who author is. No use of word 'I'. Text is in style of magazine article or advert. |
| Informal vocabulary and phrases – 'didn't have a clue' – use of slang. | No slang used. |
| Use of 'you' to make reader feel involved. | Use of 'you' to make reader feel involved. |
| Content focused on one person's experiences – not much detail on what computers can do. | Content focused on what computers can do for everyone – much more like a list of features of computers. |
| Text laid out in continuous stream – no bullet points or subheadings. | Text uses bullet points, subheadings – like leaflet or information text. |

**Sample: comparing written styles**

This is a very open question. To gain highest marks you will need to be organized in your response, and show a close attention to language. Look at how you might compare the language of the two texts, with a paragraph for each:

Text A shows us someone who didn't know much about computers becoming confident. Adam Woodyatt says that when he was at school he was fascinated by computers, but 'I didn't have a clue what I was doing'. His style is quite informal and friendly, and this helps readers to feel that computers are not just for technical whizz-kids but for people like them. For example, he says 'didn't have a clue' rather than something more formal like 'didn't know' or 'didn't understand'. Adam Woodyatt sometimes addresses the reader directly – 'You just point the mouse to what you want...' – and this makes us feel more involved, as if he is reassuring us that we can also use computers like him.

Text B also uses fairly informal language: 'Once you're connected you'll find there's plenty to do...'. The language here is like conversation in a way: 'you'll' and 'there's' are the kinds of words we might expect in everyday speech. Like Adam Woodyatt's article, text B makes the reader feel involved. For example, it says: 'you don't have to worry about the complexities of how computers communicate with each other – you just point and click on your PC.'

# Broader Answers

pages 109–118

## Letters

Your work will be assessed on the quality of your Reading.

These two letters are written for very different purposes. Analyse and explore the similarities and differences you notice between them – in who they are written for, what their purpose is, and the language they use. (Reading 16 marks)

Your answer might include the following points:

| *Text A: Lucia Lawson letter* | *Text B: Save the Children letter* |
|---|---|
| Audience: her mother. The writer seems quite close to her because she writes about her worries and calls her 'Darling Mummy'. | Audience: less specific. It is aimed at unknown readers and tries to make them get involved in the letter by writing 'Dear Friend'. |
| Purpose: chiefly this is a personal letter written to inform. It is also helps the writer to express her worries rather than keep them to herself. | Purpose: to persuade – layout has image, subheadings, short paragraphs, all to keep us reading. Uses facts to shock us, and narrative (Erisa's story) to show us how people are suffering – aims to get the reader involved in the issue. |
| Style: quite informally written – 'I'm' rather than 'I am'; '&' rather than 'and'; 'haven't' rather than 'have not'. | Style: quite complex language ('displaced', 'alleviate') implies that it is aimed at educated readership. Dramatic, sometimes emotional language – 'massacre', 'threatened' – to emphasize the horror of the situation. |

**Sample: looking at written style**

Writing about written style is something many students find hard. Take a look at how this student has tackled this aspect of the question:

1st paragraph on A

The informal tone of text A gives a strong sense that the writer is close to her mother. The date is written in a casual way – as if this is a note rather than a formal letter. The writer also begins and ends her letter in a very informal way – in particular, 'Love and kisses' is the way we would conclude a note to someone we know well. The language is quite informal, too: 'I'm' rather than 'I am'; '&' rather than 'and'; 'haven't' rather than 'have not'; plus some vocabulary which is quite chatty – 'fed up', 'really isn't much fun'.

2nd paragraph on B

detail on style and vocabulary

The writer of text B uses a more formal style. This is appropriate as the writer is addressing readers they don't know personally. The writer aims to get us emotionally involved by addressing us as 'Dear Friend'. This suggests that we are already supporters of the charity – or at least people who would probably want to be supporters. The writer writes to 'you', in an attempt to draw us in. To get us involved in the stories of Erisa and Celestine, the writer shows how terrible their life is. He uses quite dramatic words to help us to imagine this: 'massacre', 'wracked', 'painful death'. These details are shocking to read and come as a surprise after the factual tone at the start, which described what a rehydration sachet could do.

detail on style and vocabulary

# Section 3

# Student self-help sheets

STUDENT SELF-HELP SHEET 1

# Writing leaflets

### What can I do to prepare for the exam?

Study some actual leaflets. You can pick them up from hospitals, doctors' surgeries, supermarkets, and many other shops. Look at how they are put together and make a list of design features and writing styles.

### What if I'm hopeless at art?

It doesn't matter. You won't gain any marks in English for your drawing skills. Just map out how the leaflet should look and label it clearly for the examiner. For example:

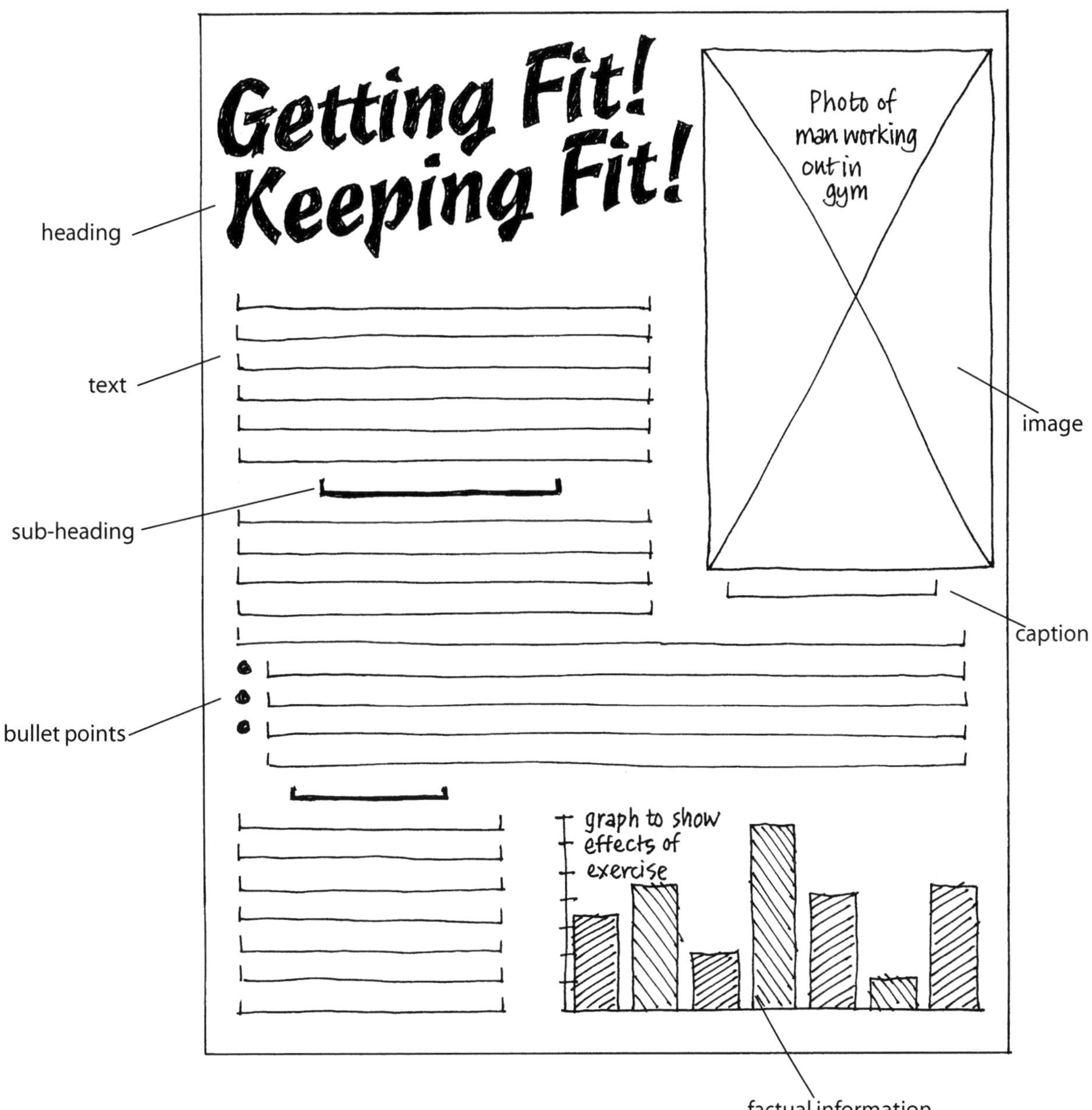


### What is the key to success?

Keeping a clear sense of who your audience is and writing for them – it needs to feel like a leaflet, not an English essay!

EXTRA PRACTICE SHEET 1

# Writing leaflets

Create a leaflet giving people of your age-group advice on ONE of the following topics:

- how to look after a certain pet; OR
- ways of improving the environment of your neighbourhood or school.

Produce your leaflet on one side of A4 paper.

## Planning

- Choose the topic you know most about.
- Notice that the first choice is an **informative** leaflet – you're expected to give information.
- The second option is more **persuasive**: you're expected to change people's attitudes and get them involved in taking more care of the environment.
- Use specific information – for example, details of a pet you have kept; or an environmental project you know about.
- Look back at the RSPCA and Greenpeace leaflets in the Students' Book – pick out any advice they give and use this in your own words.

## Language hints

- Keep your language clear and straightforward. Don't clog sentences with too much description.
- Use a variety of sentences – short and longer; simple and complex.
- Use some emotive vocabulary to get a response from your reader (for instance, use emotional words like 'pain', 'pride', 'disaster', 'pleasure').

## Design hints

- Map out a simple but clear design first.
- Don't spend too much time on drawings – get the shape of your design worked out and then get writing.
- Keep text clear and direct.
- Use a chatty tone, if that feels suitable.
- Use bullet-points, subheadings, headlines.

STUDENT SELF-HELP SHEET 2

# Writing articles

Writing a good newspaper (or magazine) article isn't easy. Journalists face limits of time (deadlines) and limits of words – a complex article may be just 500 words long and required by the editor in a couple of hours.

Remember that there are different styles of newspaper articles. The main two are **news** and **features**.

## News articles

A news article reports an event. It usually contains:

- a headline
- a strapline (adding more detail about the story to the headline)
- an opening topic sentence which summarizes the whole story to get the reader involved
- short paragraphs explaining who... where... when... and what happened
- subheadings to help the reader follow the story and to break the text up
- quotations from people involved in the story.

Sample opening paragraph:

At least ten people were killed in an avalanche during a school hiking expedition in Southern France yesterday. During the night rescue workers were searching in the snow for two more.
*The Times*, 24.1.98

who what where when

## Features articles

Newspapers and magazines also include many features articles. These are often about issues which aren't directly in the news. Writers can therefore sometimes write in a less factual style, using a different type of sentence to start. Main features are:

- a curious or attention-grabbing opening sentence
- subheadings to help the reader follow the story and to break the text up
- quotations from people involved in the story.

A feature article will aim to interest the reader in the story throughout, rather than try to give us the full account at the beginning.

Sample opening paragraph:

When Simon Vickers had his first Chinese meal in Britain after nearly 20 years in Hong Kong, he was sick. At Chinese New Year he will be more careful where he eats.
*The Times* 24.1.98

subject | attention-grabbing first sentence | leaves us asking who is Simon Vickers?

See Self-Help Sheet 3 to look at newspaper layout.

**STUDENT SELF-HELP SHEET 3**

# Newspaper layout

You may be asked to study or write a newspaper article. It helps if you know the main features of newspaper design and the technical terms to label them:

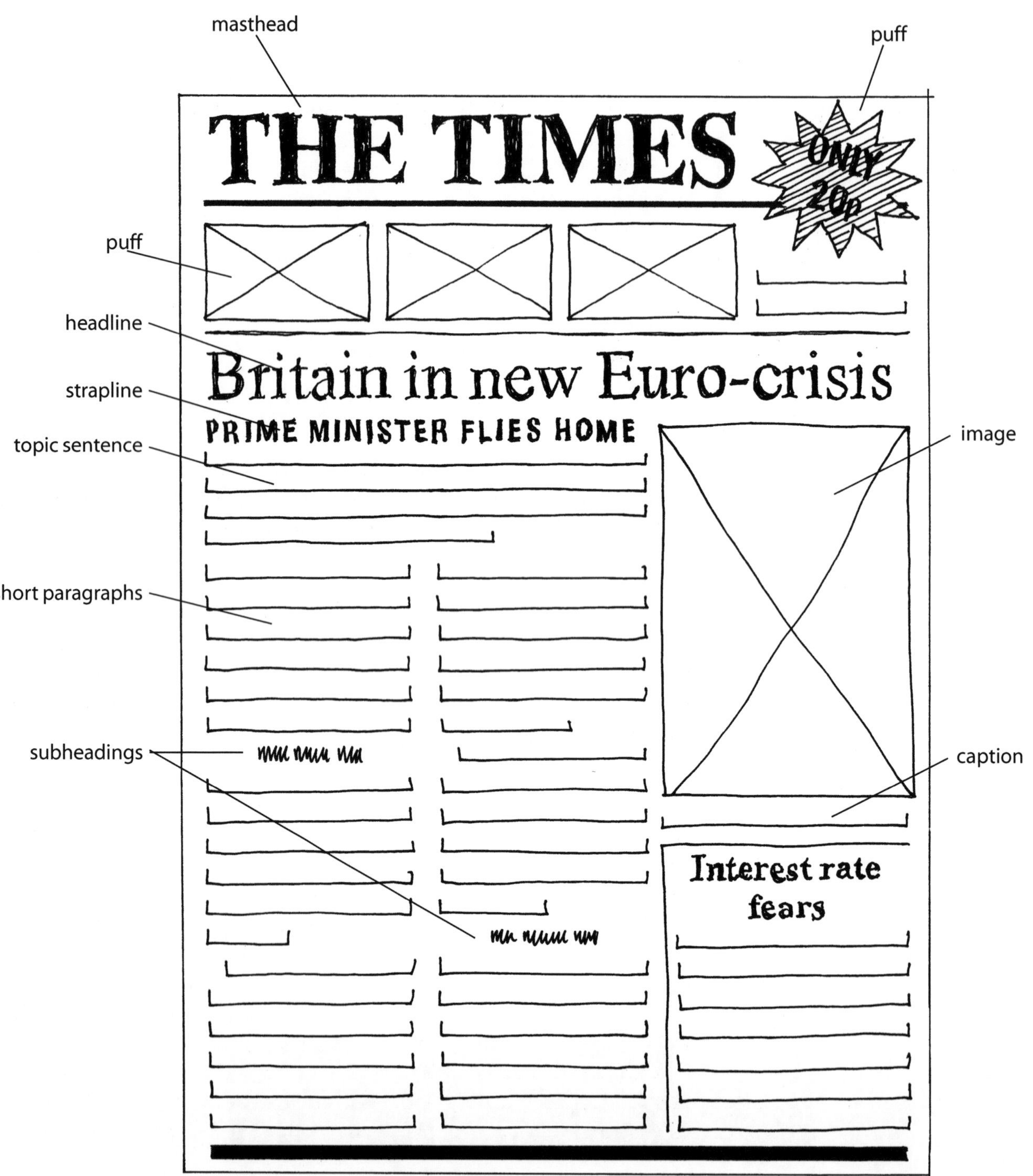

EXTRA PRACTICE SHEET 2

# Writing newspaper articles

Write a newspaper article based upon an incident in a class text you are reading – for example, the scandal at the Birlings' household in *An Inspector Calls* or the killing of Curley's wife in *Of Mice and Men*.

OR

Imagine a aircraft has narrowly missed crashing into your school or college. Write a newspaper article describing the event.

## Planning

- Get the topic right – using either the suggestions above or, in discussion with your teacher, another story which would make a good news item.
- Decide whether you are writing a tabloid or broadsheet piece – look back to pages 38–43 in the Students' Book to see how their styles differ.
- Decide whether you have to just write the story, or whether you are also designing the page – in which case it's important to think about layout, too.
- Get different elements of the story together – including some eyewitness accounts to make it feel more realistic. (If it is based on a text, have characters from that text say what they saw.)
- Remember that the headline and first paragraph aim to grab the reader's attention: spend time getting these right.

## Language hints

- Adopt newspaper headline styles. Because of pressure of space, newspapers use a compressed form of language. Headlines often leave out auxiliary verbs and other grammatical words (e.g. 'Car Stolen in Revenge Attack' rather than 'A Car was Stolen in a Revenge Attack').
- Copy newspapers' use of dramatic vocabulary – 'bid', 'crisis', 'attack', 'shock', 'horror', 'outrage', 'anger', 'fury'.
- Start your newspaper article with a 'topic sentence' which aims to tell the reader the 'who, where and when' of the story (e.g. 'A 42-year-old father of two narrowly escaped death yesterday as he was caught in a freak avalanche').
- Add details in the rest of the story (e.g. 'Roland Sunley of Colchester was walking in the Chilterns...').
- Copy the way newspapers label people – by job, age, status (e.g. 'rock star Tina Turner, 58...', 'experienced teacher, Rick Nettleton, 35...').
- Use quotations from eyewitnesses to bring your story to life (e.g. 'Daughter Tracey said, "I've never seen anything like it. One minute he was on the hill walking the dog, the next he was covered in snow..."').
- Use subheadings and short paragraphs to keep your text moving.

STUDENT SELF-HELP SHEET 4

# Writing letters

Sometimes you may be asked to write a letter in response to something you have read. You need to be clear about the audience for your letter – is it someone you know or not? If it is, you may be expected to produce an informal letter. If not, a formal letter is better. If in doubt, go for the formal style.

**Features of a formal letter**

- Your full address
- Date
- Name and full address of the person you are writing to
- Formal opening: 'Dear Ms X' or 'Dear Sir'
- Formal style of writing ('I wish to complain about...' rather than 'I'm really annoyed about...')
- Formal conclusion: 'Yours sincerely' if you know the name of the person you're addressing; 'Yours faithfully' if you began 'Dear Sir or Madam'
- Your full name at the end

**Features of an informal letter**

- Your full address
- Date (may be written more briefly – e.g. June 7th)
- Less formal greeting – e.g. 'Dear Jay'
- Less formal style (e.g. 'hope you're keeping well' rather than 'I sincerely hope that this letter finds you in good health')
- Less formal conclusion: 'All the best' or 'Best wishes'
- Your first name at the end

STUDENT SELF-HELP SHEET 5

# Letter layout

This is how formal and informal letters should look on the page:

**Formal**

**Informal**

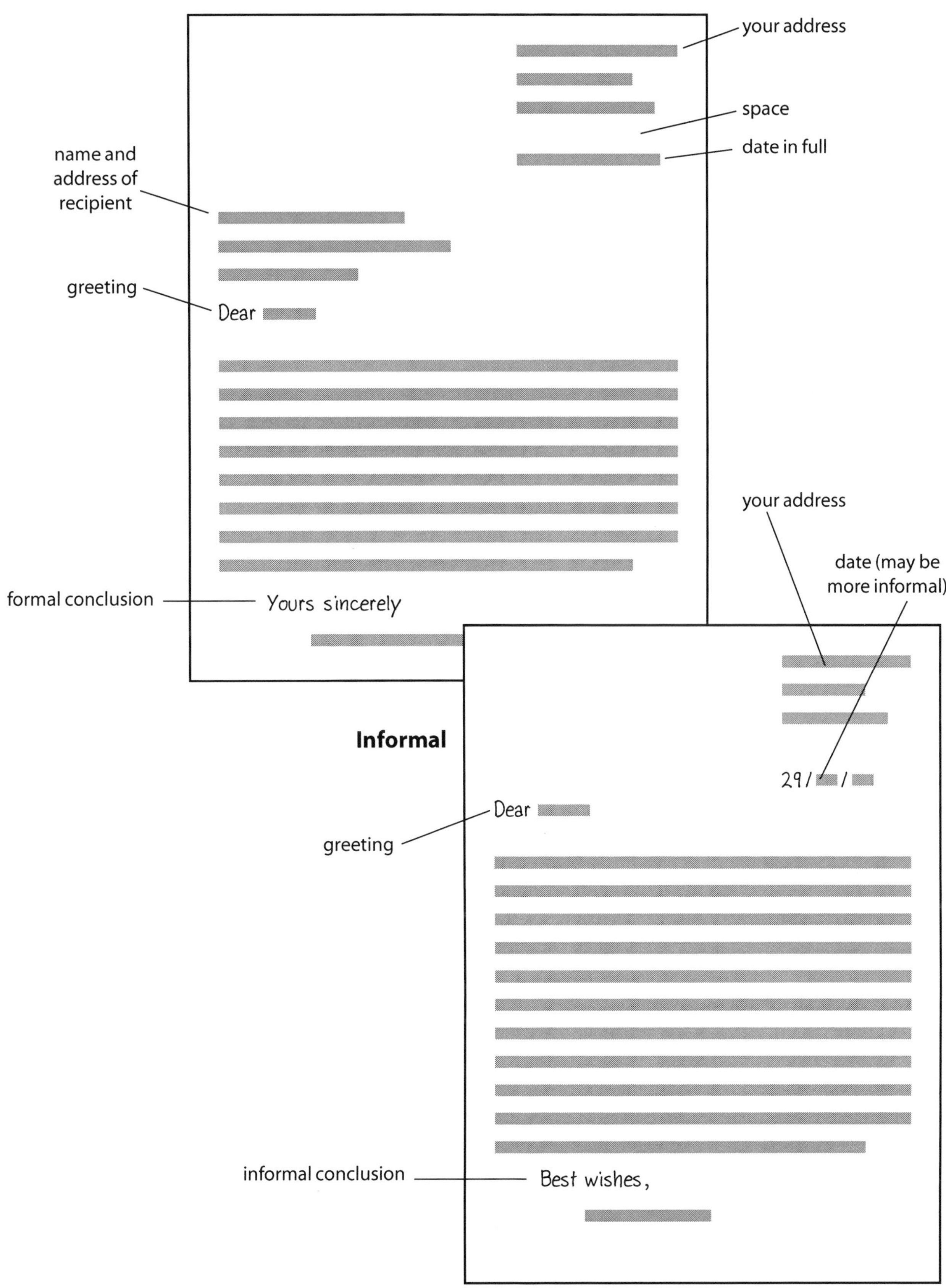

EXTRA PRACTICE SHEET 3

# Writing letters

Choose one of the topics below and write a letter in the appropriate style:

- a letter of advice to someone in the year below, suggesting ways in which they can improve their work in GCSE English; OR
- a campaign letter to the local council arguing that your school should not be merged with a neighbouring school to save money.

Aim to write one and a half to two sides of A4.

**Planning**

- Think carefully about your audience and purpose here. How well do you know the person you are writing to? This will have a bearing on the style you use.
- Get the layout of the letter right – addresses, date, the correct form of address and the correct sign-off. (See Self-Help Sheet 5 for more guidance on this.)
- For both letters, you need to plan how you will organize your ideas. Do a quick paragraph plan of, say, four to six points, so that the structure of your letter feels logical and easy to follow.

**Language hints**

- If you know the addressee well, you can afford to use a more informal style. Otherwise keep it formal – avoid chatty vocabulary; keep your sentences well controlled, rather than rambling; avoid elisions (write 'do not' rather than 'don't').
- Terms of address:
  *Informal:* 'Dear Sam,' concludes 'Best wishes,'
  *More formal:* 'Dear Mr Higginson,' concludes 'Yours sincerely,'
  *More formal:* 'Dear Sir,' concludes 'Yours faithfully,'.
- If you work on the campaign letter, remember that your aim is to persuade. Use sentence rhythms and vocabulary repetitions to create an effect like a speech – a powerful piece of persuasive writing.

STUDENT SELF-HELP SHEET 6

# Writing memos

Memos are communications usually sent between people who work in the same organization. Staff at your school will probably send and receive memos. They are brief notes asking people to do something, or reminding them of a decision. Their style is usually less formal.

**Key features**

- Heading giving the company or organization name
- Note of who the memo is from and who it is to
- Subject of memo, as heading
- Date
- Message

Sample memo:

Nettleton Enterprises

**MEMO**

```
To:      Ken Nettleton
From:    Caroline Ratcliff
Subject: Advertising budget
Date:    1.6.98

Ken,

We agreed when we met last week that you would check
the advertising budget. Any news on this? I've got a
few suggestions for ways that we could improve our
current campaign and would like to talk them through.

Are you free Monday 9.6 at 10?

Caroline
```

STUDENT SELF-HELP SHEET 7

# Writing a fact sheet

Occasionally at GCSE you might be asked to write a fact sheet based on a passage you have read. The test here is to see how much of the text you have understood and whether you can present the main points.

There are several ways of approaching the task. One active technique is to underline key ideas in the passage as you read them. This will help you to decide which parts of the text you need to refer to in the fact sheet.

Try to summarize ideas in your own words, not just quoting them exactly as they are presented in the passage.

Try also to make your written style snappy. Use sentences and even bullet-points to keep ideas grouped together. Remember your audience – and give your writing a light but not too chatty tone.

Sample fact sheet:

**Surviving exams: the facts**

Don't leave exam preparation until the last minute. Start several months in advance, training as if it were an Olympic sport you were taking part in.

Make a clear plan of what you need to revise and when you will do it. Create a realistic timetable, building in breaks as rewards for study. Try not to spend more than one hour revising for any subject at a time.

Revise actively. You need to do more than just re-read your notes. Summarize them, draw diagrams, say them aloud, ask someone to test you on them... anything so long as it's active.

Don't panic about the day of the exam. Everyone is terrified that they'll forget everything, or that they'll have left some vital equipment (pen?) at home. So long as you've been preparing for the exam over a long period, you won't need to panic.

Expect to be horrified when you first see the exam paper. Of course there will be questions there that are difficult, and maybe some that you cannot answer at all. Just try to stay calm and systematic. Plan your approach – and get started.

STUDENT SELF-HELP SHEET 8

# Writing advertisements

Sometimes you might be asked to write an advertisement for something you have read about. This is a test of your ability to understand what you have read, and to write in an appropriate style.

Remember that advertising can use a whole range of styles and it's important to think about what form you're being asked to use. For instance:

A **radio commercial** will need a short, snappy piece of text lasting 30 or 60 seconds when performed. It might be description, narrative or dialogue. But it will need to be lively and easy to follow so that it suits the audience – who may be listening in a car or whilst working.

A **newspaper or magazine advertisement** can use more text, but it will need to catch the reader's attention, perhaps using a witty or unexpected headline. Remember to write in short paragraphs to keep the reader's eye moving down the page.

The starting-point, once you know which form of advertising you're being asked to use, is what your message is. What are you being asked to say about a product or service? What is its key selling point – the feature which will make people want to have it? Once you know this, you should build your advertisement around this message.

The best advertisements take risks – so try to write something which is lively and creative. Try to avoid some of the clichés of advertising (for example, phoney conversations between people discussing double glazing, or clichés like 'You know it makes sense' and 'Simply the best').

EXTRA PRACTICE SHEET 4

# Writing advertisements 1

### Writing campaign advertisements

Look at either the Samaritans or Sight Savers advertisements in the Students' Book, pages 64–70. Use the factual details in each and devise your own advertisement for a new target audience – either the Samaritans ad aimed at young women readers, or the Sight Savers ad aimed at 11–14 year olds.

### Planning

- Sketch the layout in rough – you don't have to spend too long making it look attractive.
- Think of an image which will grab the attention of your audience.
- Think of a slogan.
- Which facts from the original will you use?
- How will you change the text?

### Language hints

- Use emotional language to gain the reader's sympathy.
- Remember that telling a specific story – for example, the story of one victim's life – can hook the audience's interest.
- Bear in mind your target audience – don't over-complicate the language.

EXTRA PRACTICE SHEET 5

# Writing advertisements 2

## Writing advertorials

Write an advertorial promoting your school or college. Write as if it were an article in a newspaper – but with the aim of encouraging parents to send their children to your school.

### Planning

- Think about the selling-points of your school or college – what are the features which will attract parents?
- Keep the audience clearly in mind – it is the parents you are trying to attract.
- Plan a rough layout to look like a newspaper article – including headline, subheading, main image.
- Decide what the image should be – one which will give the right impression of your school or college.
- Think of an approach or 'angle' you will use in the article – what will be the central point of the story? A student who has got outstanding results? A new building that has just been opened? A music concert that received rave reviews?

### Language hints

- Remember that to be successful you'll need to create the layout and language rhythms of a newspaper article.
- Look at the newspaper articles and advertorials in the Students' Book to sharpen your understanding of the genres.
- Remember that newspapers are keen to entertain as well as inform: keep your style light and lively by using snappy vocabulary and – like the Norwich Union Direct example in the Students' Book – word-play ('Aisle' instead of 'I'll').
- Keep the paragraphs short and fast-moving.
- Make up a quotation from your headteacher or principal to make your advertorial sound even more realistic.
- Be sure that your main message is communicated – you should probably end with a contact address and telephone number for parents to use.

STUDENT SELF-HELP SHEET 9

# Writing a diary

Sometimes you may be asked to respond to a text by writing a diary entry for a character who appears in the passage. To gain top marks, you need to develop a good idea of what the person is like:

- what she thinks
- how she feels
- her opinions and attitudes
- how she uses language.

Remember that diaries are written for ourselves rather than a wider audience, so they usually have an informal style. Try to make the tone of your diary match the tone of the text you have read – this will help the examiner to see how well you have understood not only the content of the text, but also its style.

**Diary layout**

Usually you just need to put down the date and then start writing. (Look for clues in the original text about when it took place – avoid putting today's date unless you are told to do so.)

Don't write 'Dear Diary' – it sounds false.

Sample diary entry:

June 19th 1945

Another terrible day. I don't know how much longer this strain will last, but it seems endless...

STUDENT SELF-HELP SHEET 10

# Writing factual reports

Sometimes you may be asked to write a factual report – for instance, a report on your work experience placement, or an account of a school event like an important match or a play.

It's possible to approach these subjects as if you were writing an autobiographical or personal account. However, if you've been specifically asked to write an factual account then it's important that you don't just write about what happened to you ('I... I... I...'). Try to stand back from events and describe them so that an outside reader can visualize them. In particular:

- describe people and places
- use dialogue to show what people said
- try to capture the atmosphere of events
- decide what are the most important stages of the event you are describing – don't just launch in to writing a list of events which took place. A factual report needs to have a structured, controlled feel to it.

**Language hints**

- Aim to create an attention-grabbing first sentence.
- Use a variety of sentences – short and longer; simple and complex – to hold your reader's interest.
- Use words which help the reader to visualize the scene – colours, textures, movements – just as you would in a strong piece of narrative writing. No one ever said that a good report shouldn't have a creative and precise use of language.

STUDENT SELF-HELP SHEET 11

# Writing autobiography

If you are asked to write a piece of autobiography, the chances are that you will be given a title or a suggested starting point – for instance:

- earliest memories
- best memory
- worst memory
- a time you were humiliated
- a time you won something
- a time when someone or a pet died
- a time of change – for example moving schools.

If you are asked to write about more than one event, choose a range of ideas and emotions to write about – this will give your writing more variety than if you write about memories which are all happy, or all funny, or which contain similar emotions.

Spend some time brainstorming ideas – don't just write down the first memory that comes to mind.

Structure your account. Remember, you might not want to start at the beginning of the memory – you might want to begin in the middle or even at the end.

**Language hints**

- Remember that personal writing comes to life when you give the reader a strong impression of the people and places you are describing – use vivid language to bring them to life.
- Aim to create an attention-grabbing first sentence.
- Use a variety of sentences – short and longer, simple and complex – to hold your reader's interest.
- Experiment with ways of avoiding saying 'I' and 'me' all the time.
- Use dialogue to show what people in the past said – even if you can't quite remember. This will help to add interesting texture to your writing.

STUDENT SELF-HELP SHEET 12

# Writing travel writing

If you are asked to write a piece of travel writing, your main aim should be to try to create a powerful sense of place so that the reader feels she is there with you. Don't just write an account of what you did on the journey: instead, think about the people you may have met and the places you saw. Think about ways of bringing your memory to life. Which people will you describe? Which experiences? Brainstorm memories before you begin to write.

In particular, aim to describe what happened without writing something that sounds too much like a list ('then... and then...').

Finally, remember that travel writing doesn't necessarily have to be about exotic locations, far-flung places, and new cultures. It might be about something very familiar – such as your daily journey to school.

**Language hints**

- You'll be using the pronoun 'I', but try not to start each sentence in the same way. The subject of many sentences will be the place or other people (e.g. 'Edinburgh is...'). This will give your writing greater variety and interest.
- Choose your words carefully, so that each one conveys a powerful picture or emotion to the reader.
- Try to use words which help to describe what you can see, hear, smell, taste, or feel – really concentrate on the senses.
- Like Michael Asher in the Students' Book, use metaphors ('a savage sand-storm punched into us with hammer force'). These will help bring your writing to life.

STUDENT SELF-HELP SHEET 13

# Writing biography

You may be asked to write either of two different kinds of biography: one where you choose the subject and do your own research in advance; or one where you are given some details about a person and you have to expand it into a longer piece of biographical writing.

If you can choose your subject:

- Choose an interesting subject. Someone who has been around for a few years will probably have more to say than your best friend.
- Work out your interview questions in advance, but don't stick ruthlessly to them – if an interesting subject comes up as you are talking, keep asking questions about it.
- Preferably, record your discussion – it makes it easier to copy up later.
- Carefully choose a range of times or experiences from the subject's life, so that you give your biography more interest.

If you've been given some facts about a person's life and asked to write a short biography:

- Pick out the key details from their life – the main events. You may not want to put down all the information you've been given.
- As with a biography you research yourself, carefully choose a range of times or experiences from the subject's life, so that you give your biography more interest.
- Try to create an interesting opening sentence which will grab your reader's attention.
- You might use subheadings to show different phases of the subject's life – for example, 'Childhood', 'Early Career', 'Later Career'.

## Language hints

- Use the third person mode ('she' or 'he', rather than 'I').
- Try to bring people and places alive using description – in the way that James Mills does in the Students' Book.
- Don't feel that you have to follow the person's life in sequence. You might begin by describing them at work; then do a flashback to their childhood. You decide how best to structure the biography.
- Remember to keep changing the pace, so that you hold the reader's interest. Move from telling the story of the person's life, to describing the background, to giving some dialogue to show their opinions.

STUDENT SELF-HELP SHEET 14

# Summarizing and simplifying

SEG students in particular may sometimes be asked to summarize a text or to simplify it. This means reading it carefully, spotting its main points, and then presenting them in your own words. That last point is important: when you summarize a text, you need to show that you understand it by using your own words, not just pick key phrases and sentences out of the original text.

### How to begin

Once you know that you'll have to summarize a text, read it through with that in mind. Read actively, using a pencil to underline key points as you go through, or writing number 1, 2, 3, and so on alongside the text to show the main ideas.

### Next steps

Then skim through again to make sure you haven't missed any of the main ideas. Now it's time to write up the summary. Think about who your audience is. If you're being asked to write for a young audience, you might use a different style from writing for an older audience. Whoever you're writing for, you'll need the style to be clear and easy-to-follow.

### Language hints

- Use your own words rather than just lifting all the words from the text.
- Keep the style formal – avoid using slang words (unless the exam paper tells you to do so, which would be unusual!).
- Choose words which will suit your audience – for instance, you may create a faster-paced, more informal style for a younger audience.
- Remember that even the most complicated ideas can usually be simplified if you write in shorter sentences, giving a step-by-step feel.

STUDENT SELF-HELP SHEET 15

# Revision guidelines

*Comprehension to 16* has been designed to help you prepare for the reading and writing elements of your exam.

**What should I be able to do?**
Read carefully and notice what texts are about, how they are structured and how they are written.

**What do you mean by 'structured'?**
How texts are organized – how one idea follows another. A story or an autobiography will often use a chronological structure – one event follows another to tell a story. Other non-fiction texts – like leaflets – don't usually tell stories and they will be organized differently.

**What if there are words I can't understand?**
Don't worry. It isn't very likely – the texts are carefully chosen, so you're sure to understand most of it. But if there are one or two words that you aren't familiar with, don't panic. Just try to work them out from the context of the whole text.

**Am I allowed to express my own opinion?**
Yes – examiners want this and you will gain marks for having your own ideas.

**Does this mean I can say what I want?**
No. Any point you make will need to be supported with evidence – preferably with a carefully chosen quotation. Examiners want to know your opinion, but it's important that this is rooted clearly in the text – so don't just make up wacky ideas!

**What should I do to get top marks?**
Pay close attention to language. Be confident about commenting about a writer's style, tone (serious, comic, sarcastic, direct...), sentences, and vocabulary. Writing about language usually gets the highest grades.

**How can I revise?**
Keep reading for pleasure: people who do best in reading papers are those who enjoy reading anyway. Be analytical about everything you read. Ask yourself about how the text is constructed, what the style is like, what the writer's purpose and audience might be, and so on.

And good luck.

STUDENT SELF-HELP SHEET 16

# General hints for answering shorter questions

## 1 Read, read, read

Students who do best in GCSE reading papers usually enjoy reading. Athletes prepare for important competitions years in advance. You should treat your examinations in the same way. Don't assume you can turn up on the day, read a text, and give it a full, considered response. You'll read it more carefully if you're used to reading all kinds of texts carefully – so read newspapers, autobiographies, magazines, short stories... as many types of texts as you can.

Chiefly read them for pleasure, but try to be analytical, too. As you read, ask yourself: who is this text by? Who is it aimed at? What is its purpose? How is it written? What do I think of it? In this way you'll sharpen up your reading skills.

## 2 Planning

If you are asked to read a number of texts and write paragraph (or more) answers to each one, use the mark allocations to guide you. For instance, if one question is worth 32 marks and another is worth 16, you should spend most time on the one that gives the most marks.

Remember also to plan your answer. Candidates who do best generally write a quick (five-minute) paragraph plan. This helps you to avoid panicking, or rushing into an answer. It sends out positive signals to the examiner that you're in control of what you're doing – and you'll end up writing a much better response.

You may be asked to choose a topic and write. You might be writing a letter of complaint, or writing a leaflet, or writing an article. Remember to plan it out first. Think about who your audience is and what you are trying to achieve. Try to set the text out so that it looks like the genre you're using. Write as creatively and as accurately as you can – and, if possible, try to enjoy what you're writing. It will make a difference.

STUDENT SELF-HELP SHEET 17

# General hints for answering broader questions

## 1 Read, read, read

Students who do best in GCSE reading papers usually enjoy reading. Athletes prepare for important competitions years in advance. You should treat your examinations in the same way. Don't assume you can turn up on the day, read a text, and give it a full, considered response. You'll read it more carefully if you're used to reading all kinds of texts carefully – so read newspapers, autobiographies, magazines, short stories... as many types of texts as you can.

Chiefly read them for pleasure, but try to be analytical, too. As you read, ask yourself: who is this text by? Who is it aimed at? What is its purpose? How is it written? What do I think of it? In this way you'll sharpen up your reading skills.

## 2 Secrets of success

Plan before you write. The questions are quite open-ended which means they encourage you to write about your observations, thoughts and feelings at length. You are frequently asked to compare two texts, and to do this well you need to structure your answer systematically, so make sure you spend five minutes or so producing a brief paragraph plan. This will help reduce exam nerves, help you to write more clearly, send out positive messages to the examiner that you're in control of your ideas – and make you feel better.

STUDENT SELF-HELP SHEET 18

# Planning an answer

Planning what you are going to write is the most important step in getting a good grade. The students who do best always organize their ideas clearly and logically, so that the examiner can follow the answers with ease.

People like to plan in different ways. That's fine – you develop the system that's best for you. But the important thing is that you have a clear idea of where you're heading with an answer before you set off writing it.

One of the most common ways of planning is to put together a brief paragraph plan. Here you think what your main points will be and label them. In a shorter answer there may be just one or two paragraphs per question. For broader answers there may be five or six paragraphs.

First write your paragraph headings – a word or two on what each paragraph will be about (e.g. 'style', or 'layout'). Then, under each paragraph heading, jot down the two or three points you will make in that paragraph.

With practice you should be able to construct a plan like this within five minutes. It will look like this:

Sample plan:

'The writer suggests that adults should pay more attention to the views of their children. How does she persuade us to believe this?'

1 layout = letter
- makes it more direct & personal
- allows her to address us by name

2 children
- makes them seem grown-up
- shows that children today are different from in the past
- says we should take them more seriously

3 adults
- says we don't have time for children any more
- we forget what they're really like
- makes us feel guilty for ignoring needs of children

4 language
- uses emotional words about children – 'innocence', 'heartache', 'suffering'
- uses harsh words about adults – 'emotionally strait-jacketed', 'cold'

5 conclusion
- layout, ideas and language all contribute to the effect
- writer v. skilful at making us take notice